SECRETS

OF

...as to be renewed o...
the last date b...

WOMEN
ENTREPRENEURS

SECRETS

OF SUCCESSFUL
WOMEN
ENTREPRENEURS

SUE STOCKDALE

First Published In Great Britain 2005
by Lean Marketing Press

www.BookShaker.com

Typeset in Georgia

Helen Swaby photograph by Tina Hadley - www.tinahadley.com

This book is dedicated to people who passionately believe that they can achieve more but don't know how to begin.

THE DUKE OF EDINBURGH'S AWARD

A proportion of the profits from the sale of this book have been donated to The Duke of Edinburgh's Award...

The Duke of Edinburgh's Award is a programme of activities for young people that develops commitment, fitness, confidence and life skills, as well as positively engaging them in their local communities. There are around quarter of a million young people between the age of 14 and 25 currently taking part in the UK, just over half of whom are young women. They come from all social and cultural backgrounds and are of all abilities.

The Award is challenging and it's fun. Taking part equips young people for life and work and inspires many of them to achieve more than they previously thought they were capable of. Sales of this book will help more young people to experience the challenge of the Award, possibly helping them to become entrepreneurs of the future.

CONTENTS

"ARE YOU THE NEXT GREAT ENTREPRENEUR?"

☐ Do you like making your own decisions and being in control of your own destiny?

☐ Do you feel passionately about an idea, product or service?

☐ Are you happy to work longer hours for a smaller initial income while you build a brighter future?

☐ Have you spotted an untapped gap in the market that you believe you can fill?

☐ Can you handle the pressure and responsibility of running your own business?

If you answered yes to 2 or more of the above questions then learn from the mistakes, challenges and successes of others when you read *Secrets of Successful Women Entrepreneurs*.

This book is for those who want to start–up or grow a business, and are fascinated to learn what drives people to achieve exceptional performance. It provides an insight on how to think like an entrepreneur, overcome challenges and become more resourceful – and enterprising.

You will be motivated to take action yourself after reading about the experiences of ten women from across the UK who all seized an opportunity and turned their ideas into reality.

ACKNOWLEDGEMENTS

The idea for this book began during a conversation over lunch two years ago. Since then, I have followed the Seven Steps to Success to see it through to completion.

I would like to thank all the people who have been involved during that time and whose support and encouragement has been invaluable.

Charlotte Howard for planting the seed in the first place, Tracey Jefferies for being a great friend and networker, Frank Martin for helping to shape the research, Sarah Williams and Peronel Barnes for their contacts and editing skills, Debbie Jenkins and Joe Gregory at Lean Marketing Press who have been a great team to work with, Fiona Hoggard and all the team at The Duke of Edinburgh's Award, Steve McLauchlan who has been very helpful, Rae, Bruce, Jenna and Connor Howieson and Michael Zarutsky who have continuously supported, cajoled and encouraged me to achieve my best work.

And lastly, to all the inspiring women who so kindly contributed to this book: Linda Bennett, Josephine Carpenter, Julie Meyer, Michelle Mone, Dr Marilyn Orcharton, Geetie Singh, Dr Glenda Stone, Penny Streeter, Helen Swaby and Yvonne Thompson CBE.

FOREWORD

Secrets of Successful Women Entrepreneurs is a mega–dose of inspiration – I felt like I'd had 5 cups of coffee all at once! It profiles 10 exceptional women entrepreneurs, who are inspirational not because of where they are now – but how they got there and why. Every woman will be able to relate to these women's stories in some way. The book illustrates how multi–millionaires like Linda Bennett and Penny Streeter started with no money and high levels of risk aversion – not unlike the profile of the ordinary women who come to Prowess members for business support.

All of them had potentially fatal setbacks at one time or another – like Michelle Mone having her new collection stolen just days before a crucial show and Geetie Singh's business loan falling through just after she signed the lease for her gastro–pub. What sets these women apart is the ability to pick themselves up, learn from their mistakes and keep going.

Interestingly wealth in itself is rarely the driving force: almost more powerful is a compelling vision, strong sense of social value and desire to deliver real quality. That balance is creating real wealth and our economy needs a lot more women like them. Sue Stockdale has clearly structured the book to enable readers to apply these experiences to their own plans. It's a practical book which should lead to real action and many more women entrepreneurs.

Erika Watson
Executive Director, PROWESS
The UK Association of organisations which support women to start and grow businesses

INTRODUCTION

There are many successful female entrepreneurs in the UK, yet most are not well known. Is it because most of the entrepreneurs who capture the media's attention are male? Or is it down to the small numbers of women who are actually running successful businesses? Whatever the reason, my motivation in writing this book is to redress the balance a little.

Research in 2004 showed that just 14% of businesses were wholly owned by women but encouragingly, numbers are on the increase. The UK government introduced a Strategic Framework outlining a number of priority areas aimed at accelerating the process of business start–up. One of these priority areas is to provide role models, hence another reason for this book.

In my business I spend most of my time helping corporate leaders and owner/managers of small businesses to improve what they do. I often use storytelling as a way to motivate and inspire them. There's something magical about reading or hearing about someone else's experiences that makes us connect with their situation in a unique manner. Stories take us beyond the glitz and glamour of an individual's success and help us understand how people achieve things that they often did not think were possible.

The true stories of the women in this book do just that. They are aimed at helping us understand how one can turn the dream of owning and running a business into a reality. All the women could be described as extraordinary because they have all seized an opportunity, and, with determination and commitment, turned it into a successful business. Yet they could also be described as ordinary because while they have pursued their dreams, they have all had to battle with the day to day challenges that face the rest of us – making sure we have enough money to survive, feeding our children and juggling the many different priorities in our lives.

Several themes began to emerge as I carried out my interviews. For a start it appears that most of these successful women started up their companies based on a different set of values and principles to the traditional entrepreneurial values of power, financial success and status. They tended to be more focused on interaction with people and helping others. Ironically, they still achieved financial success but they took a different route to get the same outcome.

All of the women I interviewed possess qualities of self–belief, focus, tenacity, decisiveness and competitiveness. They also have a strong desire to control their own destiny and the way they run their companies reflects their own personal values. However, two big challenges faced most of them – finding finance and managing some type of balance between their work and their personal life.

As leaders they behave in a manner that promotes genuine concern for others, team—working and openness which fits in well with their personal values of respect, integrity, ethics, honesty and a passion for excellence. Let me introduce them to you in alphabetical order:

Linda Bennett – Shoe designer and Founder of the shoe and clothing retailer LK Bennett who was recognised as the Veuve Clicquot Businesswoman of the Year in 2004.

Josephine Carpenter – Josephine took her passion for fruit smoothies and founded The Big J™ in 1999. She has successfully turned it into a multi—million pound business retailing worldwide.

Julie Meyer – Corporate high flyer Julie launched First Tuesday in 1999 and then Ariadne Capital. She is recognised as one of the Top 30 most powerful women in Europe.

Michelle Mone – Michelle is a Scottish success story. She founded MJM International and transformed the lingerie sector with her Ultimo™ bra and other unique designs.

Dr Marilyn Orcharton – Marilyn created Denplan, the UK's leading dental healthcare scheme and is recognised as one of the 300 "Leading Women Entrepreneurs of the World".

Geetie Singh – Award winning organic gastro pub owner. Geetie created the world's first certified organic gastropub in London.

Dr Glenda Stone – Glenda came from Australia and showed us how making things better for women could become a competitive asset. She founded Aurora Gender Capital Management that works towards the economic advancement of women.

Penny Streeter – Rhodesian born Penny was determined to be successful following one business failure. She did it in style and now heads up Ambition 24 hours which was recognised as the fastest growing unquoted company in the UK in 2002.

Helen Swaby – Helen turned her hobby into a multimillion pound art publishing business. DeMontfort Fine Art was recognised as one of the fastest growing unquoted companies in the UK in 2002 by the Sunday Times Virgin Atlantic Fast Track 100.

Yvonne Thompson CBE – Yvonne started the first known black–owned and run PR agency ASAP Communications. She also founded the European Federation of Black Women Business Owners and now works extensively in the community helping to give organisations access to minority audiences.

I created a framework called the *Seven Steps to Success*™ around which their stories are retold. These are the steps I believe are critical to success, not just in business but in achieving any challenging venture. Each step addresses key questions as explained below.

Seven Steps to Success™

Step 1 – The Defining Moment
What prompted the business start–up in the first place?

Step 2 – Understand your environment
What was happening in the marketplace and in their lives at start–up?

Step 3 – Create your own compelling vision
What was the vision that drove them to succeed?

Step 4 – Prepare for success
What were the personal qualities that helped them to succeed?

Step 5 – Start the journey
What have been their biggest challenges and how did they overcome them?

Step 6 – Maintain fitness and focus
How did they keep motivated and balance work/life issues?

Step 7 – Reach your goal – what next?
How did they measure success and what are their plans for the future? What advice do they have for other entrepreneurs?

Personally, as someone who has represented Scotland in athletics events, completed an MBA, participated in four expeditions across some of the world's most challenging terrain and started up my own business venture I reflected upon the key issues I had encountered during each activity. These steps focus more upon the *softer* issues related to motivation and mindset rather than the *hard* tasks we have to carry out.

I make no apologies for this. There are already many good business books which offer advice on how to write a business plan or create a marketing strategy – but not so many that actually model people making a difference right now.

The Seven Steps to Success™ give you the big picture on how to think like an entrepreneur, overcome challenges and become more resourceful – and enterprising.

I hope that the inspiring stories you read on the following pages will encourage you to consider starting up a business yourself. Or if you are already an owner/manager I hope it will provide some useful lessons that you can apply to your business.

I would like to thank all of these amazing women for their willingness to be open and honest and to share all their experiences – good and bad – so that others can learn.

PART 1: TRUE STORIES FROM GREAT FEMALE ENTREPRENEURS

Linda Bennett

**SHOE DESIGNER AND FOUNDER OF
THE SHOE AND CLOTHING RETAILER,
LK BENNETT**

*Recognised as the Veuve Clicquot
Businesswoman of the Year 2004*

Key Information

Business: Designer shoes, accessories and clothing

Started business: 1990

Location: 50 outlets across the UK and Paris, France

Turnover in 2004: about £45 million

Employees: around 500

Awards include: UK Footwear Awards in 2002 and 2003, Ernst & Young Entrepreneur of the Year Awards 2002 – Consumer Product Category, Veuve Clicquot Businesswoman of the Year 2004

Website: www.lkbennett.com

WHAT WAS THE DEFINING MOMENT?

Linda has always been passionate about shoes and this has influenced her career over the years. As with many young people, Linda was unsure which direction to take after leaving school. She started out taking a business–related degree but then went on to study the history of art before deciding to embark on a career based around a product about which she felt truly enthused. Apart from wanting a career that she enjoyed, she felt this would give her an advantage in business. The product was footwear and she took herself off to world–renowned Cordwainers College in Hackney, London to begin a course in shoe design. The course taught her how to make a shoe but had no emphasis on running a business which Linda realised would also be important.

In order to both finance her studies and learn about running a business Linda was managing and buying for a fashion store whilst studying two days a week at college. This juggling act was particularly difficult. Young people today also face this issue of trying to balance study time with earning an income, and many try to make some extra cash by working in the evenings or weekends which makes studying all the more difficult.

Still driven by her desire to become a footwear designer, Linda went off to France for a few months of work experience in the design studio of world famous shoe designer Robert Clergerie. This experience taught her how the design and manufacturing process worked. Armed with some newly acquired skills, Linda attended the international footwear fair held in Dusseldorf. It was during her visit there that Linda had her defining moment.

Linda could see that there were many shoe factories making high quality shoes but lacking in design content. She began to see that she could design shoes and have them manufactured in Europe enabling her to compete in the UK market where she planned to open her own shops.

Linda believes that gathering as much relevant experience as you can prior to starting up your enterprise is really important. As well as her retail experience, she had had other jobs including drawing up plans for an interior designer. She suggests, *"If you are thinking of setting up on your own, it is important to learn as much as you can from jobs relating to the industry you are interested in. However, if you feel you have learnt enough to start your own business, then it is important to be brave enough to make the leap."*

WHAT WAS THE MARKET SITUATION AND YOUR PERSONAL SITUATION AT START–UP?

Starting up a business in 1990 was tough. Britain was in the grip of a deep recession and money was tight. People did not spend much on frivolous things like shoes.

Linda had witnessed the poor manufacturing quality of women's footwear within the UK on her college course and recognised that Italy and Spain had shoe manufacturing skills in abundance. She therefore decided to have her shoes made overseas.

Linda found that she had to be very resourceful in order to start her business. Without the finance to open a shop selling her designs, Linda decided to launch her own collection of handbags to sell in other stores. In order to find manufacturers prepared to make her designs, Linda visited some of the leather suppliers in London that she knew from her college days and they kindly offered to share their customer lists with her. That way she managed to find some handbag manufacturers and started off by designing a collection of handbags which she sold to several stores including Harvey Nichols. She also did some design consultancy for Laura Ashley who at that time had a factory in Wales making handbags.

WHAT WAS YOUR COMPELLING VISION?

Whilst this experience provided the seed of a business, it also made her realise that what she really wanted to do was design shoes and to open her own shop. Her college course had given her the technical expertise and her years of weekend and holiday work with retailers such as Whistles, Russell and Bromley and Joseph had given her an insight into how to run a retail business.

Linda had a vision of selling shoes that she would like to wear herself. She describes the LK Bennett brand as *"feminine and elegant yet quirky and fun, appealing to a broad spectrum of different women.*" She kept this vision in mind as she made her plans to open her first shop.

She was able to capitalise on her wide–ranging experience as the business began to take shape – selling, designing the store, designing the product and also managing the overall business.

HOW DID YOU PREPARE FOR SUCCESS?

At last Linda had enough savings from her design work to approach the bank for a loan. She had £13,000 in her bank account and on the strength of this and using her flat as collateral, the bank lent her £15,000 and she found suitable shop premises in Wimbledon, South West London. Linda project managed the shop fitting of her first shop. She managed to persuade the contractors to work seven days a week because the clock was ticking and every day that the shop was not trading was a drain on limited resources. The shop was completed in two weeks – a record!

On the day Linda signed the lease, she cried. She was absolutely terrified at the enormity of what she had taken on. Latterly, Linda has commented *"The best time to start up your business is when you have very little to lose. It must be even more daunting when you have a well paid job that you are giving up. However, I had recently left college and did not have particularly high expectations."*

WHAT HAPPENED WHEN
YOU STARTED THE JOURNEY?

The first challenge Linda encountered was running the business with such little working capital. She managed to persuade some of the suppliers to allow her 90 days to pay rather than the standard 30 day terms. This was how the business was financed initially. It was a case of juggling all the time and it was extremely tough.

Looking back Linda recalls this time as extremely exciting but very hard work. She focused entirely on making the business a success, doing the designing as well as the retailing. She was working 7 days a week and well into the evenings. But word gradually spread and people began to flock to the shop. Many other women entrepreneurs have found that gaining customers through word of mouth and recommendation is by far the easiest way to win business and generates loyalty too.

Because LK Bennett was launched in a recession, Linda believes that it helped her learn how to run a lean business.

As the business has grown Linda has encountered many other challenges. She feels that her career has been a huge learning curve. " *The skills one starts with are constantly being added to as the business enters different phases, for example the skills required to run a small team are very different to those required to manage larger numbers of people.*"

Even now, as LK Bennett continues to open more stores across the UK and Europe there are challenges to face. The major one, according to Linda, is risk-taking. There is a huge difference between the rent for a small out-of-town store and the rent for a flagship store in a central location. Linda is not a natural risk taker and explains that she has to be fairly sure about something before she does it.

Protection of the brand image is important to the business and this is achieved in a number of ways.

The focus is on maintaining high standards in the design of the product. *"You are only as good as your last collection."*

The LK Bennett stores are constantly being updated. It is important that the retail environment is attractive and reflects the brand.

Linda is very proud of the staff in her stores and there is an emphasis on staff training. Linda sees this as an important part of how the brand is communicated.

HOW DO YOU MAINTAIN
MENTAL FITNESS AND FOCUS?

Once an entrepreneur has been successful it can be a daunting task to maintain that success. Linda believes that her success is down to the people *in* the business and believes that it is important to surround yourself with people who are better qualified than you are in each of their specialist's areas.

Leadership style is also another key factor that can help or hinder the success of a growing business. Linda's hands–on style helps her to be in touch with both her staff and her customers.

While it was all work and no play during the initial stages of starting up the business, Linda tries to leave work by 6pm in order to spend time with her daughter. Linda works in a very intense, focused way in order to get as much done as possible in her working day. She rarely has time for lunch meetings. Even after 15 years in business Linda finds that the brand is what keeps her motivated. *"I want to make the product better and better and the brand more recognised, especially internationally"*, she commented.

REACHING YOUR GOAL – WHAT NEXT?

Each individual will measure the success of their business in a different way. While the City views financial results as the key measure for corporates, entrepreneurs also use personal factors as a measure of success. For Linda being in control of her own destiny has been crucial, although she recognises that the day–to–day pressures of running LK Bennett meant that she has not always been able to do the things she would like to have done. The reward for this has been the creation of a brand and the feeling of pride associated with managing a team of people who excel in their jobs. *"Obviously family life brings one the most pleasure but I think I always wanted to be proud of my career achievements, particularly as so much of one's time is spent at work."*

Linda also recognises the power of role models in influencing her success. *"I think that both my family and school had a positive influence on my career. At my school we were pushed to our limit which helped me believe that I could achieve something that I may have initially thought was not possible."*

"My mother is very spirited and rarely concedes defeat and I found her very inspiring. My father is an entrepreneur so he was a role model for me too. Perhaps it did not seem so terrifying to start a business as a member of my close family had already taken the same huge step."

LINDA BENNETT'S TOP TIPS

◊ One has to put all one's energy into starting a business, do not enter into it half heartedly

◊ Expect to give up some of your social life, especially at the beginning

◊ Create a unique product, or a concept that will give you an edge over your competitors, love what you do

◊ Delegate

◊ Stay focused and believe in yourself

◊ Don't give up

Josephine Carpenter

**FOUNDER, THE JUICE COMPANY
(TRADING AS THE BIG J™)**

*A smoothie is a not a charming
man it's a product*

Key Information

Business: Manufacturer and distributor of fruit smoothies

Started business: 1999

Location: based in London, selling worldwide

Turnover in 2003: £3.5 million

Employees: 18

Awards include: Entrepreneur of the Year 2004 – European Women of Achievement Awards, Marketing Innovation Export Award 2003, Female Entrepreneur of the Year 2003 – Orange Small Business Awards

Website: www.thebigj.com

WHAT WAS THE DEFINING MOMENT?

Josephine Carpenter always knew she would run her own business. From an early age she has always been tenacious and confident and at the age of thirteen had three jobs. While other children were singing with a hairbrush like a wannabe pop star, Josephine was practising writing cheques!

She had a traumatic childhood, and it was because of this that she began to realise that, *"if you are going to do well in life then you are not going to get any help from others so you have to do it yourself."* This self–reliance and drive to succeed, combined with her ability to turn an idea into reality, helped her develop a talent for selling.

Josephine felt that in order to achieve her dream of "Josephine Carpenter, Managing Director" she would have to earn respect and success through hard work.

As a child, Josephine was very health oriented. She used to come home from school and mash up raw eggs, bananas, milk and peanut butter to whiz up a fruit smoothie in her mum's blender. As she got older, Josephine chose not to drink alcohol and began to get frustrated that the only soft drinks that appeared to be available in pubs or restaurants were cola, orange juice or water. She became absolutely convinced that there was a market for fruit smoothies as an alternative soft drink.

WHAT WAS THE MARKET SITUATION AND YOUR PERSONAL SITUATION AT START-UP?

In 1998, when she began to research the market, Josephine found that there was nothing like this available in the UK. The fact that the media seemed to be full of stories about diets and healthy eating, and that fast-food restaurants were beginning to offer healthy alternatives to consumers led Josephine to believe that this was the right time to launch her business.

Josephine acknowledges that while she was inexperienced, the drive to make money and succeed was too strong to ignore. She would spend hours on the internet doing research into where she could buy raw materials and how to run a business. She found out all about the US market in fruit smoothies and felt sure that it would only be a matter of time before the concept was brought to the UK.

At the time, Josephine had a good job working for a health and safety company, with all the attached benefits of pension, company car and good salary. Yet she decided to resign and took an evening job at a financial printing company working from 4pm to midnight. While she had taken a massive salary cut, this job gave her 24 hour access to the internet as well as an insight into the world of corporate business. The company printed documents for mergers and acquisitions and often lawyers would be there for hours, proof-reading documents. Josephine would talk to them about companies and shares, which she found valuable although she knew that, as she was the receptionist, the lawyers probably only viewed it as idle chit–chat.

When money began to get tight, Josephine eventually shared her business idea with a couple of friends. They were interested so she borrowed £10,000 from each of them to incorporate the company giving them each 1% equity stake in the business for their commitment and trust in her idea. Josephine felt that she had now well and truly started her business.

WHAT WAS YOUR COMPELLING VISION?

Josephine's vision was driven by the lack of availability of a product. She wanted to be able to go into a hotel room at 3am and open up the mini bar and find an alternative soft drink to cola, orange juice or water. Her knowledge of the places where she could not get an alternative soft drink drove her to consider selling to those sectors of the market including airlines and the food service sector.

Yet this unswerving belief that people would want to buy fruit smoothies and her passion to make the business work took its toll on her life. She was now working all day on her business, then switching to her evening job at the printers until midnight. Sometimes she would go home and then carry on with the business. She was exhausted but driven to succeed.

"My sister would bring me round dinner on a little foil plate because she knew I would not have eaten. Some days I did not actually get dressed and I would be in my pyjamas at my computer all day just putting things together. I probably did as much as a company with five or six employees could achieve. I was putting in 110% effort because I had no choice and no money."

HOW DID YOU PREPARE FOR SUCCESS?

Josephine wanted to learn more about the US market in fruit smoothies, so she decided to take a trip over there to find out more. She learned that the most successful juice bar chain was a franchise operation based in California. In other states such as Utah she learned that the large population of teetotal Mormons played a major role in increasing sales. The relatively low cost of building rents and raw materials along with the sunny weather were all factors to be analysed. It did not take Josephine long to do the sums and work out that this formula would not work in the UK.

What she decided to do was produce smoothies using the format of crushing frozen fruit up in a blender with some juices, so that she could sell this into restaurants, hotels and catering trade. It was not going to be cost effective to open up a stand–alone juice bar and she knew that she could not afford to compete directly with the retail sector, so Josephine identified a gap in the market and aimed to attack it.

Josephine approached a company in the US and bought frozen fruit from them and put it into little pouches. The idea was that when it was opened it would produce one smoothie to order.

There was only going to be one chance to succeed and Josephine knew she needed to launch the product at a major catering trade show held in Birmingham. She enlisted the help of all her family including her brother who is a paramedic and her brother–in–law who is a fire–fighter. Even her sister who worked for an IT firm in the City gave up her job for a week and they all became the face of The Juice Company at the trade show!

"For all intents and purposes, we were this fabulous new company and we had a real buzz on the stand with music and everyone whizzing up smoothies all day. By the end of the show we had John Lewis and Fenwick's agreeing to list our product. We won best new product of the year, which was great, yet no–one had any idea at that time that the company they were talking to was just me."

The success at the trade show led to a lot of press coverage and the business began to develop. The first year yielded a turnover of £125,000 and by end of year 2 they had reached over £1M turnover. Josephine knew that these results demonstrated there was a market for fruit smoothies.

WHAT HAPPENED WHEN
YOU STARTED THE JOURNEY?

Just like the other women in this book, Josephine also experienced her fair share of challenges. The first fruit suppliers she went to meet got up and left her sitting in the room during a meeting – obviously not taking her seriously. Nowadays if their salesmen ring her up and try to sell her their product, she makes a point of reminding them how they treated her when she was starting out. She will not buy from them on principle.

Instead she had to go out to America and bring the products back over to the UK. *"I remember the huge lorry coming down our street and as we unloaded the containers of fruit into my front room all the curtains were twitching in the street. It was hilarious."*

Another challenge she had to overcome was when a supplier "mislaid or lost" £158,000 worth of stock which they had purchased. Josephine had to placate angry customers who were waiting for their supplies while finding the money to repurchase the stock she had already bought. The subsequent months of legal wrangling meant that it took Josephine's attention away from driving the business forward.

It took her three years to really recognise the value of finding a good finance person and the importance of managing the cash in the business. When she started the business, Josephine did not have any external advisors.

Then later, when she *did* seek advice, it was not correct, so it put Josephine off asking for help from anyone else.

This issue of cash flow was brought home all too quickly to her in 2001. She had negotiated for nine months to win an airline contract. It was ready to start on 10th September 2001. The atrocities at the World Trade Centre on the following day led the airline to withdraw the contract. Yet external events like those are difficult to plan for, so Josephine had to re-mortgage her house in order to weather the financial impact on the business.

Despite all these problems, Josephine carries on because she feels a responsibility towards her employees as well as being passionate about the product. In fact, leading the people in the company is key to success, Josephine believes.

She regularly carries out an anonymous communications questionnaire asking employees to list what they like about work and what they are unhappy with in the company. The results show the strength of passion for the business. The office is completely democratic and employees are encouraged to sit round the table and talk about strategy. Everyone gets involved in designing and tasting new products, and even in how they are advertised. *"Most things are done in-house and we try not to employ outside people and because of this, they enjoy it more."* This issue of involvement may correlate with the fact that a large number of employees have been employed by the company since it started and have remained loyal.

Her plan was to focus initially on the UK market. Before she knew what had happened, The Juice Company was selling to 12 airlines worldwide and selling into the USA because the brand was so popular. They won the best new product in the airline industry within one year of entering the sector and they have succeeded in every target market that Josephine has identified.

HOW DO YOU MAINTAIN
MENTAL FITNESS AND FOCUS?

The pressure of work has taken its toll on Josephine's personal life. She took only four days holiday in the first four years of trading and acknowledges that she does not really have a life outside work. Finding it hard to switch off and relax appears to be a common challenge for most of the women interviewed. Recognising this issue, Josephine sought to address it by getting a dog. *"I bought Oscar to stop me getting so self–obsessed. If I take him out for walks I can still do my work later but it helps. At least walking the dog is good exercise."*

REACHING YOUR GOAL – WHAT NEXT?

Josephine's drive to succeed has encouraged her to set a long–term turnover and net–profit goal for the business and she has got an exit strategy at the back of her mind. Yet she acknowledges that, even if she sells the business, she will probably set up another one as being an entrepreneur is her lifeblood. *"The business needs to become an established brand and I need to create a management team so that I can go on holiday and things will run themselves. It takes time to establish that in a business."*

Josephine admits that it has been a steep learning curve for her and The Juice Company. *"I would not trust people as much. It has been hard for me to realise that all people are not as nice as you think they are. Also, in this industry being a woman has not helped. Some people treat you like an idiot and they always ask who owns the company because they assume it's someone else."*

Yet she would not give it up for anything. That feisty determination and confidence has shown through and undoubtedly helped the business to grow.

JOSEPHINE CARPENTER'S TOP TIPS

◊ Employ a right–hand person immediately if you can afford it. Find them from word of mouth and recommendation

◊ Trust your gut feel and act on it

◊ Believe in yourself and your capabilities

Julie Meyer

FOUNDER AND CEO, ARIADNE CAPITAL AND FOUNDER, FIRST TUESDAY

Named as a Global Leader of Tomorrow

Key Information

Business: Global investment and advisory firm

Started businesses: First Tuesday in 1999, Ariadne Capital in 2000

Location: London

Turnover in 2004: £5 million

Employees: 12

Awards include: Named as a Global Leader of Tomorrow by the World Economic Forum, One of the Top 30 most powerful women in Europe by the Wall Street Journal, Entrepreneur of the Year 2000 by Ernst and Young

Website: www.ariadnecapital.com

WHAT WAS THE DEFINING MOMENT?

American born Julie Meyer knows better than anyone how to grab opportunities and capitalise on them. On graduation from Valparaiso University in Indiana, the 21 year–old moved to France and quickly learnt to find a job and build her own network. These formative years in business clearly influenced Julie's later choice to run her own business.

"I worked in a marketing agency which was run by women and although it was not sex discrimination I experienced, it did make me learn that other people may have different agendas and may not want you to get ahead."

As she moved her way up the career ladder, Julie recognised she wanted to drive her own future and be in control rather than facing continued resistance from others who did not want her to realise her potential.

Julie decided to take a year out to complete an MBA at the top French business school INSEAD and it was during this course that she started to study venture capital. *"I had managed teams of people, but never been responsible for getting a venture up off the ground. The MBA brought all the components of business together and then it all made sense."*

Having completed her studies Julie decided to head for London. She felt in a way that, being an "outsider", she was in a better position to see opportunities than her

British classmates. They were returning home, saddled with debt, and not with the same hunger to be successful. *"Even today I try hard to keep that outsider's fresh perspective"*, she comments.

She was concerned at being out of the business world for a year but reminded herself that she had been in a similar situation once before when she had moved to France. She had got through that okay so she used her experience to help keep her focused and motivated. Julie recalls that she stopped seeing any of her friends and almost went into hibernation, although externally there was a great deal of frenetic activity as she met people in the venture capital community. It was this intense level of focus that she believes helped her succeed.

"What I noticed about trying to get into the venture capital community at that time was that focusing on what I would bring to the table I got people to meet with me. They recognised that there was a knowledgeable source of information because they perceived me to be already inside the industry even though I did not know anyone or have a job."

Good fortune struck when Julie landed a job as Assistant Director at New Media Investors just in the midst of the dotcom boom. This involved helping to raise funding for the likes of lastminute.com.

WHAT WAS THE MARKET SITUATION AND YOUR PERSONAL SITUATION AT START–UP?

The dotcom boom made Julie hungry to make her mark. So in October 1999 she launched First Tuesday, so called because it brought together Net entrepreneurs and investors on the first Tuesday of each month in around 70 cities across the world. Spawned from an idea of using networking to bring people together, it gave Julie first–hand experience of running a business.

It was a real challenge, and although Julie acknowledges she made some classic mistakes with First Tuesday, it all contributed to her ability to learn from it and move on. *"You need to be able to let things go and move on, otherwise you get caught up in the emotional cycle. I have learnt to forgive myself for making mistakes."*

As she became more steeped in the world of venture capital she saw a lack of accountability and integrity from many people in the industry. She felt driven to launch a venture capital business that would offer those things.

WHAT WAS YOUR COMPELLING VISION?

Her vision for Ariadne Capital was to build a powerful brand with a purpose. She wanted the company to be known as innovative and for entrepreneurs to say that Ariadne are good backers to have, for investors to say that Ariadne choose the best people to back and for her to have the best team possible.

HOW DID YOU PREPARE FOR SUCCESS?

After the sale of First Tuesday in July 2000, Julie recognised that she would have to move quickly to catch the public's attention, in order to bring her dream to fruition. The industry publication at the time, The Industry Standard, put her on the front cover saying "Goodbye First Tuesday, Hello Ariadne, the net's next business model", which gave her a good start because it helped people to understand that this was a new business venture she was focusing on.

Over several months, from a blank sheet of paper, they raised $3 million dollars from investors. Bearing in mind that the dotcom bubble had burst by this time, Julie says, *"It was unusual at the time to say I have got this idea and it's worth $3 million, at $15 million valuation, and get people to back you."* Yet the reputation that Julie had built obviously paid off and the 21 investors who came on board recognised that there was a real benefit in being part of Ariadne Capital.

WHAT HAPPENED WHEN YOU STARTED THE JOURNEY?

After the First Tuesday experience Julie quickly learned to become more selective about the people she got involved with and also how quickly she got involved with them. She paid great attention to identifying individuals with the right skill–set and focused on looking for people who had start–up operational experience, deal structuring skills, and who were interested in technology and knew how to sell. It took her a while to build the right team and the she went through a number of iterations.

Her approach to finding good people has been based on believing that you will attract them to your business. *"You need to be who you are and keep on finding ways to broadcast out who you are and what you believe in, what you expect of people, what your standards are and what you value. You allow people to self-select themselves into your orbit. It's not about writing a job description but about standing for something whereby people say I want to work for that."*

The issue of gender does play a role in how she views her team too. Julie feels that many women have a high "internal bullshit detector" and that they don't try to kid themselves about their actions. She feels that some men can have a problem with their ego, which just does not allow them to see things clearly, to act quickly or to build relationships.

"I certainly have an ego but I am able to leave it at the door every morning to get stuff done and as long as it does not affect my confidence or have people walk all over me, I feel I am more efficient, a better leader and it's an advantage."

HOW DO YOU MAINTAIN
MENTAL FITNESS AND FOCUS?

Julie is firmly convinced that we can all create the future we want to live in and she uses this as a guiding principle. In other words, our actions will be driven by putting something in first before you expect anything back – rather like the principles of networking!

She believes that if you focus on what you bring to the table and how you can create value then you are not fooling yourself. Her deep sense of integrity shines through all the actions that she takes within the business. *"If we create things that are valuable, people will want to buy them (as in businesses) and others will get capital gains or returns."*

Success does not come without hard work though and Julie clearly is committed to putting in the necessary hours to achieve the results she wants. She asks a lot from herself and expects a lot from her staff, but demonstrates this through leading by example. Her leadership style could be described as inclusive and she strives to ensure that employees have the opportunities to make a greater impact at Ariadne.

Julie likens it to a basketball team. *"I am the captain of the team but I want a team of stars. At any moment you might get the ball and you have to be able to make the shot but there is always the captain who has to make choices and take responsibilities. Sometimes the captain is not the most technically skilled person but they can lead. That's how I see this organisation."*

This hectic lifestyle offers little time for relaxation. And while family doesn't appear top of Julie's agenda currently she feels that her maternal urge is focused on the company. *"I hope it doesn't sound condescending but I do feel maternal affection for the people here, so whatever void that fills in my life I am happy. I am glad that I am able to contribute something to make this world a better place and if I can be a role model of a businessperson with integrity then that's satisfying."*

REACHING YOUR GOAL – WHAT NEXT?

Ariadne Capital is clearly focused on success. Julie measures her success not only in financial terms but also in terms of repeat business. She also views interest from possible future purchasers of the business as another measure of success. Yet Julie knows that underpinning all the financial results are the people who contribute towards delivering the end goal. She recognises that she is passionate about helping them to grow and develop as individuals, and describes a "moral compass" within her and tries to encourage people around her to achieve continually higher standards.

JULIE MEYER'S TOP TIPS

◊ You know more than you think you know

◊ Don't allow people to tell you you are not good enough to be CEO. Come to your own conclusion by critically evaluating your own skills

◊ Listen to your gut feel and you will pick up a lot about people and opportunities

◊ You need to be attentive to small details because together they can indicate the bigger picture

◊ Be careful about the relationships you get into and be prepared to walk away from things when there is not a win–win

Michelle Mone

FOUNDER, MJM INTERNATIONAL,
DESIGNER OF THE ULTIMO™ BRA

Key Information

Business: Lingerie designer and retailer

Started business: 1996

Location: based in Glasgow and Hong Kong

Employees: 48 in Glasgow and additional staff in Hong Kong

Awards include: Business Start Up of the Year 1997, Entrepreneur of the Year 1999 & 2000, World Young Business Achiever 2000, Business Woman of the Year 2000 and Great Scot of the Year 2000, Voted one of the Top 35 Women in the UK by Management Today in 2005

Website: www.ultimo.co.uk

WHAT WAS THE DEFINING MOMENT?

Michelle Mone, from Glasgow, is one of Scotland's most well–known entrepreneurs. She seized an opportunity to help women look sexy when she came across an advert in a US magazine for breast enhancers and subsequently created the Ultimo bra now worn by housewives and celebrities across the globe. Yet her journey to become an entrepreneur began in less enticing surroundings.

She grew up in the East End of Glasgow, traditionally a working–class area. Her father worked in a factory and her mother was a machinist. Tragedy hit the family when she was 10 years old when her brother died of spina bifida. It affected the entire family and made Michelle suddenly grow up because she was the only child now. She began to lose interest in school and woke up every morning wishing she was older so that she could earn money to help support the family.

She did start work delivering papers and then grabbed the idea of helping one East End fruiterer to market his produce. At the time there was fierce competition and one of the shop owners appeared to be struggling, so Michelle convinced him to let her help. Over the months Michelle began suggesting changes like putting fruit out in front of the shop and discounting produce that was bruised or going bad. His business began to turn around thanks to Michelle's marketing skills.

When she was 15 years old, her father woke up one day in pain. He began to limp around giving the impression he was drunk but he was unaware that he had a serious problem. Two months later he was paralyzed from the waist down. This put even more pressure on Michelle to bring home an income and she decided to leave school and see about getting a proper job.

Michelle recalls the pressure due to lack of money. "*It was my 14th birthday and I really wanted a stereo but mum explained that she only had £5 in her purse. She decided to go to the bingo to see if she could win and arrived back with a huge stereo because she had won £500 on the day of my birthday. It was fantastic.*"

Michelle started modelling as a way to earn money and during this time she met her husband. They got married when she was 18. Now that she had additional responsibilities, and recognising that modelling did not provide a reliable income, she got a job as an office junior with Labatts, the Canadian brewer. By the time she left the company, when they closed down six years later, she was Marketing Manager for Scotland and was the mother of two children.

While taking a well–earned break with the family in America, Michelle read a story in a magazine about a US manufacturer who was making gel breast enhancers to go inside your bra. Having breast fed two children, she was desperate to regain her cleavage, and so set out to find the manufacturer during their holiday. Michelle then spent the following two months tracking down the manufacturer. Once they identified who it was they went over and presented their idea to the company. Initially it was going to cost £150,000 to win the European licence, but after three days of negotiating, the company gave it to Michelle at no charge. This was the moment when Michelle's dream of running a business was about to become a reality.

WHAT WAS THE MARKET SITUATION AND YOUR PERSONAL SITUATION AT START-UP?

This concept of breast enhancers was completely new to the UK and so the first thing Michelle did was arrange a meeting with Rigby and Peller, famous for their made-to-measure corsetry, to show them the idea. The owner thought they were amazing and immediately gave them an order for 400.

Michelle thought it would be a great idea to incorporate these enhancers in a bra rather than them being removable. This proved too costly at £150 each. In addition, the enhancers were not washable. Over the next three years Michelle found a team of scientists in Germany who were willing to try and create her vision of the bra with the enhancers included in it, that could be safely washed while retaining the ability to mould to the shape your breast. The scientists eventually came up with the solution and Michelle prepared to launch it onto the market.

Two weeks before the planned launch, Michelle moved into her offices and also gave birth to her third baby. 48 hours later she was back in the office sitting on a rubber ring and determined to make the business a success. She now regrets not spending a lot of time with her children but feels that she is now able to give them some of the things that she never got. *"I could never be a full–time mum but I love them dearly and if I have any spare time I spend it with them and not on myself."*

WHAT WAS YOUR COMPELLING VISION?

Michelle's vision for the company has always been to help women feel good about themselves. The company has continually sought to innovate and now offers a wide range of products to the customer.

HOW DID YOU PREPARE FOR SUCCESS?

Financing the business was a major issue. Her husband Michael is Managing Director in the company and manages all the detail. They used their house as security with the bank and were about to run out of money but she was determined that the business would take off. So they went to see multi–millionaire Scottish entrepreneur Tom Hunter to ask for help. His wife Marion tried on the bra and thought it was amazing and so convinced her husband to support them. In return Tom took a 20% equity stake in the business. It is just at this early stage in a business where it is at its most vulnerable. Many entrepreneurs find that they give away too much equity in their business early on in return for financial investment. The popular BBC show Dragon's Den, highlighted the difficult negotiations that many entrepreneurs have to enter into in order to gain sufficient funding for growth.

WHAT HAPPENED WHEN
YOU STARTED THE JOURNEY?

The Ultimo bra was launched in Selfridge's department store in London in August 1999 and gained the attention of the world's media. Nothing like this had been seen before and it totally revolutionised the lingerie trade. They sold 12 week's stock in just 2 hours.

MJM International has never used advertising but they do have a hugely powerful PR asset – Michelle herself. She has a love–hate relationship with the press and makes sure that she always provides them with a good story and images. In return they have mainly been supportive of her business venture. Over the years Michelle has built a brand that would have required £10 million investment to get it known worldwide and that has been achieved with zero advertising.

MJM International obtained the worldwide patent and shortly afterwards Michelle received an intriguing phone call. She remembers the lady said, '*I am Barbara Lipton, the President of Saks Fifth Avenue department store in New York. We want to stock your bras in our store.*' I thought it was a friend winding me up and so I *joked – don't wind me up today, I am really busy, and slammed the phone down!"*

An hour later an email arrived from Barbara confirming that her request was genuine. So six weeks later they launched in the US. Then they found out that film star Julia Roberts had worn the bra while filming *Erin Brockovich*, which provided additional PR and boosted sales.

Everything was going well for the business, including an offer to buy the company from a wealthy American business–woman who arrived on her private jet to discuss the proposal. Despite a generous offer, Michelle and her husband decided to carry on.

But things were to go horribly wrong. Unscrupulous companies started to copy their designs and Michelle was unable to fight back due to lack of financial resources. She decided that the only way they would be able to retain their brand would be to pull out of retail stores so that they had the financial resources to diversify. This went against the feeling of the board of Directors and Michelle had to work hard to convince them of the viability of her strategy.

"In the back of my mind I had always thought we only had one style of bra available in different colours which was gel filled. If demand tailed off we would be out of business. So I had this plan that if we developed a wider product range with over 100 different styles of gel bras

with removable inserts, sexy bras and every–day bras it would ensure our success in the longer term."

Within a year, Michelle had put together an entire collection, partly driven by the fear of losing everything, having to move to council accommodation and seeing her three children suffer. The company successfully launched Ultimodirect.com and a call centre to handle sales and gained 50,000 customers within a month. This demand was driven by the great PR they were receiving in publications such as OK magazine and on TV shows.

Debenhams Chief Executive Belinda Earl had watched from the sidelines as Michelle transformed MJM International. It had gone from a company selling one bra to a brand name offering an extensive collection. Belinda was impressed enough to want to supply their product so in October 2002 they launched in 103 Debenhams stores. At the same time Michelle signed up top model Penny Lancaster as the celebrity face (or rather body!) promoting the Ultimo products. The success of this promotion led to their products being stocked in every department store in the UK.

HOW DO YOU MAINTAIN
MENTAL FITNESS AND FOCUS?

There is no doubt that Michelle has found it tough to maintain motivation over the years while facing various potential disasters. The first was while they were riding high on their US success. MJM International teamed up with a US distribution company that had been recommended to them. Three months later they had not delivered any stock to customers and disappeared with £150,000 of Michelle's money. It took up many needless hours of emotion and energy trying to recover the debt.

Her husband had joined the company on a full–time basis and the pressure was taking its toll on their relationship. They resorted to working with Ted Anders, renowned as a coach to NASA's astronauts, who helped them to learn to speak to each other again. Many husband/wife partnerships in business find it challenging and one of the ways to respect one another is to value the diversity that each individual offers the business. Michelle's husband Michael is analytical while Michelle is the complete opposite and the outcome tended to end with fireworks.

One of the worst situations that Michelle experienced was in February 2003 when she was 'carjacked' outside her office. The assailant stole her car, which contained all her samples for meetings with next season's buyers scheduled for the following week at a trade show. They amounted to a year's worth of work that had been stolen. It nearly broke her spirit. At the time her husband, Michael was working at their office in Hong Kong and so she was left to recover from her attack at home with her children and mother for support.

Michelle knew that if she didn't go to the trade show to meet the buyers they would effectively have nothing to sell for an entire season. This was because the buyers tend to make decisions for an entire season at these events. But she could not face going along empty-handed. It was Michael, her husband who arrived back to save the day and pull her out of her depression. He had pleaded with the workers in the Hong Kong factory to work round the clock and make up similar samples to the ones that had been stolen. They achieved a month's worth of work in 4 days, which was unheard of in the lingerie business.

"I remember Michael coming back in the morning and finding me in my pyjamas on the day of the show. I said I cannot go through with this so he literally dragged me upstairs and shouted at me to get showered and dressed as he had seen enough. It was the best thing he ever did. I went down to the show and it was the most successful one we had ever been to."

Despite all these setbacks Michelle remains reflective about her experiences. *"I think that I have been put through all of the bad things in order to appreciate the good. If I only had the good I would probably be a real pain in the arse and a prima donna."*

People in business can often be motivated by sceptics and Michelle agrees. *"If someone thinks I cannot achieve it, I become even more determined to succeed."* Celebrities began to ask Michelle how they could wear a backless dress with a bra. Many of the technicians believed it was not possible but Michelle was determined not to be swayed. It eventually took 18 months to find a solution. The next stage was demand for wearing a bra with a dress that was backless and also cut to the navel. It took over a year to design. Michelle is rightly proud of their achievements. *"It's pretty amazing for a small company to come up with three inventions in three years but I never say that something is impossible."*

She is well aware of the impact that her mood has on the rest of the staff. Over the years she has realised that they pick up on her mood and tend to mirror it. So if she is feeling down, then she will choose to stay at home or arrange to be out of the office.

Michelle thinks that she is direct, yet fair with her staff. *"I treat people how I would want to be treated myself but I am a bit of a perfectionist. Some people might describe me as obsessive because I am concerned with every detail of the business. I call up the call centre and put on a different voice to hear what type of service they give to customers."*

Whatever her leadership style, the staff appear to be fully committed to their jobs. In the run–up to a huge music event and fashion show that they organised in Glasgow's conference centre in 2003 all the staff worked until 9pm continuously for two months. It brought the team together and gave them a great sense of achievement. They raised £130,000 for Breast Cancer Campaign and the Princes Trust.

REACHING YOUR GOAL – WHAT NEXT?

MJM International has had its fair share of ups and downs over a relatively short time. Michelle measures the success over that time in terms of what they have managed to achieve. *"We have built a strong brand from nothing and given customers innovative new products that are stylish and competitively priced. I don't think that I would change much if I had to start again – I am glad I have learned the lessons that I have. I'd perhaps be more careful when investing in new products."*

They now own seven other brands including *Michelle for George* at Walmart and they recently launched the big cup range with Jennifer Ellison called *Young Attitude*.

MICHELLE MONE'S TOP TIPS

◊ If your business does not work take responsibility for it yourself and don't blame others around you

◊ Don't start your business unless you are prepared to put your whole heart into it

◊ Remember all the others around you when you become successful. There are others that will need your advice so make time to offer it

Dr Marilyn Orcharton

FOUNDER AND MANAGING DIRECTOR
OF KITE CONSULTANTS, DEVELOPER
OF ISOPLAN AND FOUNDER OF
DENPLAN

*Created the UK's leading dental
healthcare scheme*

Key Information

Business: Professional Services

Started businesses: Denplan in 1986 and Isoplan in 1997

Location: Glasgow

Turnover: £3 million

Employees: 12

Awards include: Elected as first woman President of the Glasgow Chamber of Commerce in 1998, Winner of TSB's "Women mean Business" Best Newcomer Award in 1999, "Leading Women Entrepreneurs of the World" honouree in 1999, British Dental Association's 'Medal of Honour' for Services to Dentistry in 2000.

Website: www.isoplan.com

WHAT WAS THE DEFINING MOMENT?

There was no key defining moment when Marilyn decided to start up Denplan, but her story that led to the launch of the business is fascinating. As a child Marilyn always had an imaginative mind, partly she says, because she did not have many toys or a television to take her attention, so instead she listened to the radio. Leaving school, she was interested in medicine but eventually decided to study dentistry because it seemed to offer greater flexibility.

Her imaginative mind helped her to gain distinctions in medical surgery because she excelled at diagnosis. She recalls, *"it did not matter what patient they showed me because I could pinpoint what the problem was and loved solving the clues based on the symptoms."* Marilyn excelled in dentistry and was awarded several accolades. Subsequently she was offered jobs in dentistry research but preferred to take the route into practice. As the years progressed Marilyn married and had two children and then set up her own dental practice:

At the time there were no equal opportunities in dentistry. At university there had been a maximum of five places in every fifty available to women. Even if there had been fifty women who excelled the university could not enrol them. People believed that any woman who *did* qualify would later give up when they got married.

There was also a lack of equality in terms of being responsible for your own affairs if you were married. Marilyn remembers when she stopped work in 1968 she had to stop paying her superannuation. *"At the time it did not unduly bother me because I bought a car. My husband even had to sign my tax return until 1982, which he objected to."* This lack of financial independence has been a contributing factor to many women not having sufficient financial backup to satisfy the banks when applying for funding.

During her work as a dentist in the 1980s, Marilyn saw a lot of problems with the existing systems that seemed to reward poor dentists while making life tough for the best. Marilyn couldn't understand why dentists were only paid for doing fillings and not for keeping people healthy.

The irony was that if you were a good dentist who looked after your patients and prevented problems from occurring you faced a greater risk of going out of business. And that *is* what happened to many dentists who worked under the Health Service. Marilyn just couldn't accept that it was possible for all the good dentists to go bankrupt while the public believed that they must have gone out of business because they were bad. It was this unfair situation that drove Marilyn to consider a different reward system.

Her idea was to create a system where dentists were paid to keep patients healthy. It would be like an insurance policy where patients paid around £5 a month and if they needed treatment there would be no extra charge. Marilyn compares it to travel insurance. *"People don't mind paying insurance because they don't want a plane to crash and are quite happy to pay the insurance company to carry that risk."* While Marilyn provided the imaginative concept for the business, she acknowledges that she would never have actually set up the business herself.

WHAT WAS THE MARKET SITUATION AND YOUR PERSONAL SITUATION AT START–UP?

Armed with her imaginative new system for dentistry Marilyn composed a letter to the British Dental Association (BDA) where she was involved with committee work. But before posting it she showed it to a colleague who worked in the Medical Defence Union. He immediately suggested that, rather than offer the idea to the BDA, they should do it themselves. Marilyn talked the idea through with her husband who was very supportive, so they decided to go for it and this is when Denplan was founded in 1986.

Marilyn did a lot of market research before they started and because both Marilyn and her colleague were dentists they had a lot of professional contacts. So they used their network to find an agency to do some market research. The results of the research were not entirely promising. Patients thought a dental insurance scheme was a great idea but they did not entirely trust their dentists. They were concerned as to how they would know that the dentist would give them the appropriate treatment once they had taken their money. They also wanted a win–win situation and wanted to know if there was a fallback position if the dentist treated them wrongly in any way.

Marilyn and her daughter, who was an architectural student, devised the chart to assess patient risk. If you had a lot of fillings in your teeth you were a higher risk and if you had none it would be less. This chart is now a national standard and Marilyn laughs that they did it on the back of an envelope! They also introduced lots of points for oral hygiene on the chart so if you brushed your teeth really well and looked after your mouth and gums you would come down a category. *"To this day I don't think anyone has ever done so but it provided an incentive to go and brush your teeth,"* Marilyn comments.

The business succeeded because of a good team. Marilyn's colleague was skilled in the management and accounts side of the business while she focused on getting customers in, doing the marketing and telling everyone how wonderful their product was. *"We nearly went under several times but my partner did not tell me except for when we were on the brink of bankruptcy. This was a good arrangement because I could float along doing my creative thing without worrying."*

People invested in their business because the core team had all the skills and experience required to run a business of this type successfully. Marilyn believes that one of the most difficult things in starting up a business is to find someone who has complementary skills to you to get it off the ground. When you start out in business you are not always aware of the skills you need to have. Therefore it is difficult to know what to look for in others. Her business partner in Denplan did not have her vision, but he knew all the detail behind making it happen. She believes it was just complete luck that it worked so well. *"Normally this sort of person wants a 50–50 split with the founder. In my case I insisted he was paid more because he was working long hours doing all the accounts. Most entrepreneurs don't mind what they pay these people as long as they get the job done."*

Marilyn recalls that even back in the early 80s they had management systems in place including a staff handbook and office procedures which was to be the seed for Marilyn's second business venture.

The business thrived and several years later in 1991 one of the original investors who had sold his shares wanted to buy back into Denplan. He recognised the business was growing even during a recession and he could see the long term potential. So he offered Marilyn a sum of money for her shares. By this time the business had achieved what Marilyn had wanted it to. She thought it was a perfect time to sell. *"Having come through times when I thought we would never have money again as we had not been able to pay ourselves a salary, it was wonderful to see a result.*" So Marilyn sold her shares, leaving her colleague to continue on in the business. He subsequently sold the company in 1993 to PPP for £42 million.

WHAT WAS YOUR COMPELLING VISION?

Having sold one business Marilyn was not content to relax and watch life go by. She was still haunted by the issue of public accountability. Were dentists getting better at what they did because people seemed to need fewer fillings or was it because the dentists were not doing the filling? She spent a year finding out about European systems of health delivery. Her research showed that in other countries healthcare was organised and controlled in a way that was much fairer to the public. She began to think about a way to meet this public accountability, so that the onus was on the professional like a doctor, lawyer etc. to make sure that they were doing things correctly. If something went wrong, the patient could identify where it had gone wrong because the procedure was transparent.

The internationally recognised quality standard ISO9000 was around at the time and although it had some benefits Marilyn thought that it was unwieldy. However, rather than make a judgement, she opened a small office and employed a member of staff. The two of them attended courses on ISO9000 to find out more. Then they went on lead assessor courses and acted as consultants in a bid to really understand what it was all about. Eventually Marilyn, realised that no–one fully understood it.

"People knew what the end product was but they had no idea of what the point of the process was. We realised it was just like having processes in a hotel where they have a checklist when they tidy the rooms. Fold over the toilet paper, make the bed etc. So it was just a question of a lot of checklists which of course they call audits on ISO9000. It was simply about having a plan for how things should be done and then sticking to the plan and making a checklist so that people can check how things are done."

What Marilyn realised was that many professionals were concerned that they did not have the plans in the first place. She had been trained in drilling teeth but how she did it was in her head and not written down. And while dentists had been trained in the technical areas they had not thought of applying the same principle to the management of the business. While they had an appointments book, it took a legal change to force dentists to have many other documented procedures for complaints, sterilisation and other processes.

Her vision began to emerge: to create a software tool for all professionals including doctors, dentists, and hairdressers, in fact anyone who was vocationally trained, that would enable them to document the processes in their business. In a large company there are departments who manage these issues but in a small business the owner/manager has to do it all and often this type of work gets overlooked.

Marilyn's passion for public accountability remains strong and helps to keep her focused on achieving the vision. She believes her ethical values come from her background in medicine and that this product helps to bring back some ethics into business because it gives professionals visible guidelines to work from.

HOW DID YOU PREPARE FOR SUCCESS?

In order to turn her vision into reality Marilyn needed to collect all the information from professionals about their processes. This took her team five years to complete during which time they were not generating any revenue. One of the biggest challenges was getting the software written which was very expensive and proved to be an even bigger headache than collecting the information.

They also found that it was difficult to market it to the smaller businesses who were reluctant to invest in software that they did not feel would offer any immediate return on investment. So Marilyn and her team had to sell directly to Primary Care Trusts, Health Boards and nursing homes. Marilyn acknowledges that the business only began to generate income in 1997 and it took five years before it really started to grow.

One of the challenges that Marilyn encountered in developing Isoplan was finding a suitable business partner. She knew that investors would only buy into the concept if the people were right and she found it tough to find a suitable candidate. So she invested most of her own money and then found individuals – family and friends who were prepared to invest £100K or so into the venture. The remainder came from a local investment fund and the bank.

Marilyn also used her experience from Denplan to introduce a payment plan option to the package. She then found that she was being driven by the investors to sell only this part of the package because it had a greater financial return. But she remained steadfast and refused to do so because for her the whole point was to get the quality system in place first because it was the public accountability element of the product that she was so passionate about.

WHAT HAPPENED WHEN
YOU STARTED THE JOURNEY?

During both her first and current business ventures, Marilyn encountered her fair share of challenges. Several times she has faced the wrath of the bank when there was no more investment coming in and they were not able to pay salaries. However Marilyn has overcome these challenges with a fierce tenacity and determination. She acknowledges that it has been a lot easier for her knowing that her husband was also bringing home a salary and keeping the house going.

"I have two grown–up children and grandchildren but without my husband managing the house and family as well I don't think I could have taken such risks. I would not have wanted to put my children through the financial ups and downs. I have run the businesses all on my side and got into debt but have not involved my husband as any debt was mine. I could not have done that until Margaret Thatcher changed the rules in 1982 where I was able to report as an individual. The bank only judges me and it's nothing to do with my husband."

This tenacity is also demonstrated through Marilyn's strong sense of personal belief. She firmly believes that accountability is the element that is missing from the health service and that her system will address this gap. *"I am doing this because I know there is a gap that needs to be filled. I just know that things could be made better and easier for people. This can sound very altruistic, but, if things are made better it will be better for me and my kids as well."*

HOW DO YOU MAINTAIN
MENTAL FITNESS AND FOCUS?

As a working mother Marilyn managed to juggle her work and family effectively by relying on the support of her husband during the week and then assuming the role of mother at the weekend. While she was with Denplan their office was based in Winchester because it was closer to the South East of England so Marilyn would commute there on Monday, work extremely long hours and fly home on Friday. At the weekend she would cook, clean, shop and see her family. She describes her husband as disciplined while her more creative approach to life gave her children a good balance.

In order to keep motivated over the years Marilyn has read a lot of books by other entrepreneurs. She quotes stories about other well known people who struggled initially and then overcame the odds to be successful. Even age is not a barrier to success. Marilyn explains that Walt Disney cashed in his pension to set up Disney World. It is always useful to learn from others.

REACHING YOUR GOAL – WHAT NEXT?

Marilyn Orcharton measures success by how much she is able to change things for the better. She acknowledges that Denplan changed the face of dentistry, and that many of her principles of prevention are now used by the National Health Service too. She hopes that Isoplan will improve the management of many organisations in the long term, including the NHS.

Marilyn does not see herself running this business forever. She believes her exit route from the business will be selling out to a big software house that is likely to take the product even further. Only time will tell...

MARILYN ORCHARTON'S TOP TIPS

◊ Decide what kind of person you are – an organised managerial type or a creative thinker. Know yourself and then employ the opposite

◊ Finance is key – find somebody who can manage the money. If you get a good bookkeeper they are worth their weight in gold

◊ Be prepared to take risks but don't gamble unless you can afford it

Geetie Singh

**MANAGING DIRECTOR OF
SLOEBERRY TRADING LTD**

*Founded the world's first
certified organic gastropub*

Key Information

Business: Organic Gastropub Company

Started business: 1998

Location: Two gastropubs in North London

Turnover in 2003: £2.5 million

Employees: 60

Awards include: Awarded Businesswoman of the Year Award 2000 by the Publican, London's best dining pub by the Good Pub Guide in 2002, Entrepreneur of the Year – Asian Women of Achievement Awards in 2002, BBC Mega Mela Enterprise award in 2002.

Website: www.sloeberry.co.uk

WHAT WAS THE DEFINING MOMENT?

Geetie Singh decided in 1994 to open up an organic gastropub which would combine her skills, experience and personal values. Geetie grew up in a commune in Worcestershire. Politics was the founding principle. *"We used to sit around the table and discuss politics and my opinion was valid from a very young age. We were self–sufficient in all our vegetables and they were all grown organically. We bought Fair Trade which back then was hard to do. I was taught to question and challenge the status quo."*

Geetie had a keen interest in singing and so decided to go to Music College in Birmingham when she was 16 years old. She was the youngest ever singer to attend but found the competitiveness and restrictions on her personal life unbearable at that age so she left. Geetie then found fill–in work in restaurants in London and absolutely loved it. But she was shocked to see how unsustainable they were and how appallingly the staff were treated. Waitresses were often not paid an hourly rate and had no employment rights. Kitchen porters worked 78 hours a week and just about made enough money to live on. None of the owners appeared to have thought about the consequences to their business, they were only focused on money. It took Geetie about five years to come to terms with the fact that the rest of the outside world was not like the commune she had grown up in.

Quickly Geetie was encouraged to go into the management side and although she was not keen at first she absolutely loved it. She made up her mind that this is what she wanted to do in life. However she was also adamant that whatever type of restaurant she ran it would be organic and live up to her ethical values.

But she lacked business management experience so her father advised her to go out and get all the experience that she was likely to need in the future. Geetie started by taking a job in a restaurant with a big emphasis on finance to get experience of the accounting side. Then she needed to learn about the organic sector, so she worked in a whole food shop in Primrose Hill in London. *"I used to look at all the people coming in and think, would they come to a pub serving organic food? I used to ask different people and some were very dubious about the organic side of things. But I knew that, as a normal person who drinks and smokes and eats organically, I wanted to eat organic when I went out and was sure that others would too."*

WHAT WAS THE MARKET SITUATION AND YOUR PERSONAL SITUATION AT START-UP?

As Geetie gained experience she thought she needed to find a business partner. While she had 8 years restaurant experience as a manager she had no money, but Geetie was determined to make her plan work.

She was finding it hard to put her ideas into a structured format in order to impress other people and so she rang up a friend's father for advice, explaining that she needed about £50,000 to get the business started. He provided some words of encouragement but also happened to mention that his daughter (and Geetie's old friend), Esther, would love the project but that she was busy with other things. Eventually Geetie rang her, realising that she needed to find someone who she would be able to bounce ideas around with and who could also provide some encouragement and moral support when things got tough.

Esther was to bring a different set of skills and experience to the team. Having completed a history degree at University she had begun work in the film industry. Later she moved to work in museums before doing a Masters in Museum Studies. In between she had worked in bars and restaurants and as a chef. When Geetie rang, Esther was working as an Exhibition Assistant in London.

It was an opportune moment when Geetie rang for help. They met in the Lansdowne, a gastropub in London, on a Friday and on the Monday they started to work together on the business plan. A year later they opened the Duke of Cambridge.

They both had very different skills so it was clear right from the start who would take on the different roles. Geetie's skills of staff management and front of house were different to Esther's skills of project management and administration. While they got the business going they both were involved in everything.

Gastropubs were relatively new, and only four existed in London in 1997. The formula seemed to be: buy an old pub, strip it back, and furnish it with reclaimed tables and chairs, and offer simple food from a small menu.

WHAT WAS YOUR COMPELLING VISION?

Geetie was convinced that the idea to run an organic gastropub would work. But it took a while for her to be entirely comfortable marketing the business as organic because she was worried that it would put people off coming. *"We marketed ourselves as an organic gastropub to the press and a bloody good gastropub to the public. We kept it a secret at first about the organic bit and people would come in and want to order a pint of Fosters. It was only the lack of their usual beers that confused them at first and we would have to explain we were organic, shove a pint of the beer in front of them and say taste it. People loved it."*

But deep down all the actions that she took were underpinned with the values of ethics, fairness and treating everyone with respect.

HOW DID YOU PREPARE FOR SUCCESS?

One of Geetie's first tasks was to write the business plan. Her lack of education did not deter her and she asked

Esther's father, who is a business advisor, for help in finding the information. He gave her a business plan outline checklist which included a SWOT analysis form that she used on the gastropubs that currently existed. He also encouraged her to find some market research that she could use to convince investors of the growth potential in the organic movement as well as the gastropub concept. Esther's analytical abilities were extremely useful in interpreting the market research information as it made Geetie's eyes glaze over!

Undoubtedly, the issue of start–up finance was Geetie's biggest problem. Initially she thought she would need about £50,000 but, after finishing her research, she realised it would be nearer £250,000. She planned to raise this by obtaining a bank loan and finding private investors. One of her friends initially put in £60,000. It was a huge demonstration of support and meant that she could confidently approach the banks and other investors saying she already had some funding.

No–one ever wants to be the first person to invest in a new venture and it's always a challenge to make people feel that they are not the only person taking a risk. Geetie tried to keep all the parties interested by being a little economical with the truth at times. Sometimes she had not got a final written agreement from an investor but Geetie would speak confidently as if she had the money. It was all aimed at giving people a feeling of confidence that others felt this venture was worth investing in.

Geetie visited a bank that she did not really expect to back her at the start and practiced her pitch on them. Although she didn't get the cash she got feedback that her business plan was one of the best they had ever seen. Then she went to another bank and met a really enthusiastic female business manager. She thought the idea was fantastic and agreed to lend Geetie £100,000. This support then helped her to get other investors on board and she thought it was all settled.

So now the next task was to find a suitable site. Geetie identified several and each time she attempted to get them the deals fell through, costing money on lawyers, architects and surveys. Then she found the site in St Peters Street, Islington. She had to be really sure it was viable so spent a week around the site checking out the area and assessing if it would be the appropriate location to attract her target market.

She counted the number of net curtains compared to blinds on the windows of houses. She noted the types of cars parked in the area. She even counted the different type of shopping bags that were being carried past, as well as how long it took to walk from the underground station and bus routes. All of this information helped Geetie to form a judgement about the viability of the site. Eventually she decided this was an ideal location and approached the bank with the view to obtaining the loan.

Meanwhile Geetie had told the landlord she would take the site and began the work refurbishing it to the standard that she required. A week before it was due to open, Geetie received a phone call from the bank manager who apologetically told her that the bank manager who had agreed the loan had not been authorised to do, so the money was not available.

It was a terrifying situation, Geetie remembers. "*I had come so far and spent so much money it just could not be possible that I would have to quit. So I realised I would just have to find the money one way or another.*" I spoke to all the investors and then decided I would have to tell the landlord because I might not be able to pay him. Being honest with him worked and he could see the determination within her to succeed so the landlord agreed to keep working for a week to see if she could get the money. If not he would have to delay the job for months and the business would not have got off the ground.

This is when her fighting spirit shone through. Geetie got out the business plan again and went to see every wealthy person she knew. She even went to see some of the customers that she had served in the whole–food shop, because she knew they spent over £200 per week in the store, and asked them if they were interested in a business proposition. Her work paid off and she managed to get the money she needed.

WHAT HAPPENED WHEN
YOU STARTED THE JOURNEY?

Geetie developed a good working relationship with her staff. She adopted a democratic style of leadership valuing all ideas and ensuring that no decisions were made without consulting the staff. She tried to delegate as many jobs as possible because the staff responded well to being given responsibility and control. Everyone was aware of the financial goals as well as the goals related to style, atmosphere, ambience and cleanliness.

All the systems in the pub have been created by the team. Geetie encourages staff to be open and honest. At the end of each shift they all sit down and review what happened. So if someone does not get salt and pepper on their table they can review what the system is and come up with a solution. All the changes are written down in the review book and at the end of the week they re–implement the new rules that have been created. Anyone can run this session and it does not require Geetie to manage the process. That way the responsibility is given to each member of staff.

Geetie has found that staff turnover is relatively low compared to the norm in the catering industry. Perhaps it's worth noting that staff get paid above the minimum wage, and have a bonus scheme attached to the targets they have to achieve. Geetie believes it's partly to do with the recruitment policy. *"We will only take people with the right attitude to business. I have become more ruthless about sacking people who don't fit in. I am not doing them or us a favour keeping them here."* She has no qualms about being tough but believes she tries to be as reasonable as she can be with staff. No–one is allowed to work more than 45 hours a week without getting paid overtime, which is unheard of in the catering trade.

HOW DO YOU MAINTAIN
MENTAL FITNESS AND FOCUS?

While Geetie looks after the wellbeing of her staff, she believes she needs to walk the talk in terms of work/life balance. She tries not to work more than 50 hours a week but it does not always work out. *"I remember the first time I had a weekend off. I just called Esther up and sat there saying what do we do now? So we met up and talked about work. I am completely over that now."*

One of the ways that Geetie keeps motivated is by knowing that her business is delivering a service to the community. *"We are surrounded by a residential area and I know that a lot of people have met each other through our pub. Neighbours have become good friends. We deliberately have big tables and no music so that people can sit and share and talk. It reminds me of mealtimes in the commune when I was young."*

REACHING YOUR GOAL – WHAT NEXT?

Geetie recreated her success a second time by opening the Crown in North London.

Geetie is not sure it is feasible to continue to grow the business. *"To create a gastropub of this quality requires so much attention to detail and to be able to offer this dining experience up to 8 hours at a time is challenging. I could run nice–ish restaurants in a big group but you generally don't get that attention to detail consistently. Very few people have managed it."*

It is important for her to continually find new challenges. Geetie recently went back into the kitchen to learn cooking skills along with the chefs. Success for Geetie is defined as earning a decent income in return for having a reasonable work/life balance. She also has a powerful sense of social responsibility and ethics which has helped her to create a wonderful recipe for success in the gastropubs.

GEETIE SINGH'S TOP TIPS

◊   You can do anything if you want to badly enough

◊   Always get agreements in writing

◊   You can't do everything straight away so learn to prioritise

◊   Get as much advice as you can from others before you start while having the confidence to believe in your own vision

◊   Trust in your gut instincts when making decisions

Dr Glenda Stone

**FOUNDER AND CEO, AURORA
GENDER CAPITAL MANAGEMENT LTD**

*Creator of Aurora
Women's network*

Key Information

Business: Working towards the economic advancement of women

Started business: 2000

Location: London

Turnover in 2005: £1,000,000

Employees: 8

Awards include: European Women of Achievement Award in 2002, Winner European HP Business Vision Award in 2004

Website: www.WhereWomenWantToWork.com

Aurora is an international organisation working for the economic advancement of women. It provides gender diversity software and consultancy services to corporate organisations, and a thriving 20,000 member businesswomen's network. Founded in March 2000 by Glenda Stone it has grown since then to provide services both at industry level and for individual women. Clients range from Microsoft and Goldman Sachs to PricewaterhouseCoopers and ASDA and their women's networking events for both corporate and entrepreneurial women are well attended.

WHAT WAS THE DEFINING MOMENT?

Glenda's first experience of gender issues was when she was five years old growing up in Australia. Every lunch hour the boys at school would race and take over the swings and she would think – why do they do that? Why do the girls never get the swings? Frustrated at not being able to understand this situation she fought back by rallying support from the other girls. Her strategy was to encourage all the girls to race as fast as they could to the swings once the school bell had rung and to swing for as long as possible no matter what happened.

Next day this plan was put into action, but the boys had a different tactic. In Australia the trees have spiky leaves so the boys pulled leaves off the trees and just stood there with their hands out holding the leaves so that every time the girls swung up and down their arms got scratched until they were red raw. Slowly, one by one, the girls got off, leaving Glenda as the last girl to survive. She didn't have a vendetta against boys but just realised that it wasn't fair.

Glenda grew up, left school and became a teacher in the Australian outback. She began to realise that the curriculum for girls was very gendered and patriarchal. She also noticed that some of the parents of the children she was teaching would tell their daughters that they wouldn't go to university, and that it would be better if they got married, had children and worked on the farm, in contrast to their brothers, who were encouraged to go to university.

As a twenty–one year old, Glenda had already begun to question these gender differences. She looked at the Grade 5 Social Studies curriculum for History and realised that it really was "HIStory" – there was no mention of any great women. She thought that people should be aware that things were not fair and that something needed to be done to provide equality for women.

Her teaching career then moved up through curriculum development into policy development and after a number of positions in the government Glenda eventually ended up being in the Treasury. As Assistant Executive Director in the Queensland Treasury she ran programmes aimed at the economic advancement of women and this became her passion.

There came a point where she felt that she would like to do some travelling and so armed with a few weeks leave on full pay, a rucksack and a Diners Card in her back pocket she headed for Europe.

It was during this trip Glenda realised that it didn't really matter what job you did or what academic qualifications you had, you were judged by others on whether you were a good person and could make people laugh. It was this moment of realisation where she suddenly saw that she had been a medium–sized fish in a small pond and there was a much bigger world out there that she could be part of and make an impact on.

Glenda travelled through Greece and during that time met her future husband who was holidaying with friends. They met on Santorini in September 1998 and were married the following Valentine's Day. Glenda then migrated to London and considered her next career move. She decided that she had three options; to work for the government, to work for a corporate organisation or to start her own business. The latter appealed to her most because she could develop her passion for encouraging the economic advancement of women in her own way.

WHAT WAS THE MARKET SITUATION AND YOUR PERSONAL SITUATION AT START–UP?

The market situation in 1999 was buoyant because of the dotcom boom. It was cool and groovy to go into business. Glenda felt this was the right time for her to become an entrepreneur and chose a social enterprise which was *for profit* because she believed it would also do something good for the world at the same time. She knew it was risky because she had not done it before, but she did have the safety net of her husband who was working full time. It was also risky in terms of her career because in most start–ups the owner can never initially draw the salary they were used to in the corporate world. Glenda recognised that these risks could be balanced by other benefits in terms of job satisfaction, greater drive and greater control.

Today, research shows that only 6.6% of the UK population is engaged in some form of activity that has either community or social goals at its heart. Men are slightly more likely to be involved in a social enterprise start–up, but the gap between male and female entrepreneurs is much narrower in this sector than in the "traditional" business start–up sector.

WHAT WAS YOUR COMPELLING VISION?

Glenda had a powerful and compelling vision from day one. Inspired by her work in Australia, she wanted an organisation that would change the way industry addresses women and one that would drive new practice, good practice and best practice in how industry markets to women and employs women. Her vision was to have an organisation that was totally 100% for profit. It would be a business where no–one would tell her what to do except the people who pay the money for her company to work towards the economic advancement of women.

Glenda also says, *"I wanted a snazzy organisation that would come up with new thinking and new ways of pushing the edges to make 'being better for women,' a competitive asset. This is how the term gender capital was created, because some companies have more of it than others and it's worth something."*

While Glenda is clearly motivated by achieving bottom–line results, she is also passionate about the difference that her organisation makes and states her values as *"fairness, equity and justice"*, values which are clearly woven into the fabric of her enterprise.

HOW DID YOU PREPARE FOR SUCCESS?

Being a first time entrepreneur, Glenda recognised that she needed to learn some new skills that would be beneficial in the longer term, so she started up a small web–design agency which enabled her to learn about the practicalities of business management, including the day to day issues of completing the VAT return, finding clients, marketing, managing the finances and using technology effectively. From this small beginning it took her nine months to develop the skills she needed to be prepared to launch her "real business."

Glenda used the online community she had developed from her technology experience to build her professional and entrepreneurial women's network, which was the real business she wanted to run. She named it Busygirl and launched it on International Women's Day 8th March 2000. The term 'girls' comes from Hilary Clinton's famous quote "Good bye to the old boys' network, hello to the new girls' network." Within six months it had over 2500 members.

WHAT HAPPENED WHEN
YOU STARTED THE JOURNEY?

The Busygirl network was the seed from which Aurora (as the company is now known) grew. It was a shrewd way for Glenda to understand what women were thinking and saying, where trends were going, and it gave her grass roots credibility. At the other end of the spectrum, industry recognised that Aurora had the voice and ears of women too. Women entrepreneurs also knew that Aurora had some very strong relationships with the corporate world about trying to create a better world for women to work or have a business. Glenda is adamant that they will never let go of the individual and industry levels because it's very unique. Not many companies work at both of those levels.

The first year was focused on gaining revenue from the events and training that they ran for both corporate organisations and women entrepreneurs. The second year developed into achieving increased sponsorships and becoming a channel to market for corporate organisations and conducting various services for them.

In the third year Aurora has become more focused on selling shrink–wrapped products to bring scalability to the business. Sales of their global gender management software *GENDEX* that powers the online service at WhereWomenWantToWork.com have been very successful with many corporations purchasing the application. Glenda sees this strategy as key to Aurora's business growth. *"We still retain our gender marketing services revenue stream but the software has provided an important scalable area for revenue growth."*

Glenda's gritty Australian character is prevalent in her leadership style. She makes no secret of the fact that she enjoys control and that when hard decisions have to be made for the good of the business, she has no fear of ruffling a few feathers.

"In a bad economic climate my management style is quite different compared to than if we had more resources and longer deadlines. I am a really black and white person, and I don't have time for beating around the bush, so I put everything in black clear terms. I make sure people know what their role is and make sure that they get any training they require and sufficient resources. But if they don't perform then they don't last long. I think some people imagine that if you are a woman you will be super duper nice about everything but I don't sugar–coat stuff. I make it really clear so that there are no misunderstandings and I will be very specific about the words that I use. In a small

company, when you are the boss and a woman, people can sometimes expect that things will be easier so that's a tough one. I never shy away from difficult situations."

She is passionate about creating a mutually shared vision and thinks that if people are running in different directions they will slow the business down. *"You have to make decisions about staff and that maybe someone is not the quickest person but they are reliable, and if the dynamic people go spinning off in another direction you have still got reliability to keep you moving forwards."*

From a personal point of view Glenda says she has learned to be absolutely focused, and that the key is to work less but do more. Glenda believes that you can't be everyone's chum all of the time; sometimes hard decisions have to be made because the survival of the business depends on it.

HOW DO YOU MAINTAIN
MENTAL FITNESS AND FOCUS?

Work–life balance is something that does not always feature in Glenda Stone's lifestyle. Like many of the successful women entrepreneurs I interviewed, they are driven by trying to make their business a success and are prepared to sacrifice having a social life. Generally, most socialising has to have a business context at the same time. However, it's all about choice. Glenda wants a lifestyle where she is well off and in order to achieve that she is prepared to work more than a few hours per week.

She would prefer to achieve her business goals and put her social life on hold to a certain degree.

"It's the old 80:20 rule. There are 100 things to get done and there are probably 20% of them that are the key priorities. The others just don't always get done."

As Aurora has grown, there have been new challenges to face. Glenda acknowledges that operational expenses have increased, staff numbers have increased and as they deal with more clients there comes increased responsibility to deliver results. Quality has become the big focus. The quality of suppliers and relationships with suppliers and clients has taken greater precedence.

The biggest challenge that Glenda finds is finding staff with the breadth of skills and the right attitude required for working in a smaller company. In a small business the quality of the people is a major factor in the success of the organisation.

REACHING YOUR GOAL – WHAT NEXT?

In 2002 Glenda Stone won the European Woman of Achievement Award in recognition for her outstanding entrepreneurialism. This was a solid recognition of just how far Aurora had advanced in a few years. This is, however, only one measure of success. Glenda reflects that she came from another country knowing no–one in the UK, built a very large businesswomen's network, secured an impressive list of corporate customers and managed to grow the business profitably year on year.

This is only part of the journey. Aurora now aims to be the leading provider of gender management software globally. Glenda wants companies to get better at attracting and retaining talented women. This is why Aurora wants to become the global voice on which are the best companies to work for and why. She feels this approach encourages industry to improve its strategy towards women's advancement and is a more positive approach than being critical or negative about the lack of change. Although the situation for Aurora in the future appears bright, there is no getting away from the bottom line of business. Glenda continues to focus hard on driving revenue growth. Aurora has retained all its equity and has never required funding or loans to date.

"If you don't make money, you don't have a company and then you don't have a choice, and then you have to go back and work for someone else or start all over again."

The business remains true to its values in the midst of focusing on profitability. Aurora's online service for women to research and compare companies and apply for positions is free for women, but the companies using the software that powers the site pay an annual licence fee. It's a win–win for both parties. Corporates want to get in front of career women and the career women get a highly useful research and comparison tool. At the end of the day it's a kind of poetic justice because the corporates have to become more transparent and work harder to create better working environments and business opportunities for women because the marketplace is very competitive. And the nice thing is that women win, because *they* don't have to pay a penny for it. It also helps them realise first hand the power of their collective voice, a power that has not been fully realised yet.

GLENDA STONE'S TOP TIPS

◊ Learn all the skills you will need as quickly as you can

◊ Find the right mentors from the start

◊ Be focused in what you want to achieve

◊ Focus on the money, if you don't have that you don't have a business

Penny Streeter

FOUNDER, AMBITION 24HOURS

*Created a unique model for
a 24 hour business*

Key Information

Business: Personnel recruitment and management

Started business: 1996

Location: Sutton, Surrey

Turnover in 2003: £60 million

Employees: 150

Awards include: CBI Entrepreneur of the Year in 2003, Management Today Top 100 Entrepreneurs: Top woman and No. 13 overall, Fast Track 100 'Fastest Growing UK Companies No.8 in 2003, Fast Track 100 'Fastest Growing UK Companies No.1 in 2002

Website: www.ambition24hours.co.uk

WHAT WAS THE DEFINING MOMENT?

Penny Streeter's drive to start up Ambition 24hours was led by the need to earn an income. Unlike some of the other women entrepreneurs in this book, her defining moment was finance–related rather than driven by a passion for a product or service.

Her first job after leaving school was working as a beauty therapist. She started out working for a couple of salons and quickly realised that it was more lucrative to rent space and run her own business within a hairdressing salon. Since 1985, the beauty care market was not as established as today as women were not so keen to spend money on pampering so it was a hard slog for Penny. Having decided that she wanted to focus on something else she walked into a recruitment agency to find work and was immediately offered a job in the agency itself.

It was a fairly small company where Penny learnt a lot from one of her entrepreneurial colleagues and in no time she had worked her way up to Branch Manager. So she recruited Marion, the co–founder of Ambition 24hours (who just happens to be her mother) to run the other branch and they were extremely successful between them. In 1987 it was a very competitive market. So much so that their success was earning them a huge amount of commission which displeased the owners, who thought they were a little *too* successful and felt threatened. Penny and Marion were made redundant and replaced with two cheaper (and less threatening) members of staff!

Angered by this situation, Penny and Marion decided to start up themselves and along with another partner set up a recruitment agency in Croydon.

They obtained a loan from the bank and set out to open their plush new premises, investing in state of the art furniture and equipment, only to see the housing crash of 1987 have a major negative impact on their business.

As they were still getting high–calibre people coming to their agency to register as candidates, they decided to diversify into a dining club offering dinner parties all over the country. The situation did not improve and subsequently they reluctantly made the decision to close the business. They had signed a lease for sixteen years on the premises and it was only because Penny was heavily pregnant at the time that the owner felt sorry for them and let them off their obligations.

Penny then decided to make a clean break and headed for South Africa to work with her sister, who ran a cabaret restaurant and was at the time going through a marriage break–up. However, her introduction to the restaurant business in Johannesburg was not plain sailing, and they regularly faced the threat of hold–ups or violence. Penny continued until her daughter fell ill with meningitis and she decided to return to the UK. She arrived back on Marion's doorstep, pregnant with her third child, penniless and in the process of getting divorced. Life could not get much worse! It was at this moment that Penny decided the only way to get herself out of this situation was to start up her own business again.

WHAT WAS THE MARKET SITUATION AND YOUR PERSONAL SITUATION AT START–UP?

Marion was reticent about starting up again but they decided together that if they were going to do it they would not borrow any money. That way any mistakes they made would be their own. The husband of a good friend of Penny's ran a business and agreed to give them a desk in the corner of his office to get started. Because they had no money, both of them fell back on a previous skill of working as children's entertainers, in order to pay the bills. Penny is one of four children and as a child in Rhodesia all of them had run lots of discos so when each of them arrived in the UK they had all started up this work here in order to find their feet.

Trying to look after three children and run a business was difficult, so between Marion and Penny they took turns to work one day and look after the children the next day. They found cash to pay for their advertising by running a disco and taking the cash to the newspaper and paying for it immediately so they did not incur any debt.

WHAT WAS YOUR COMPELLING VISION?

It was self–belief that drove Penny to imagine that they could be successful a second time round. Time had passed and they had analysed where they went wrong and they recognised that they had gone headlong into things, borrowing money and signing a lease, and that they had basically been naive.

HOW DID YOU PREPARE FOR SUCCESS?

The business started to accumulate some money in the bank but they took no salaries because they were fearful of what lay in the future. The little funds that they made were all invested back into the business. This fear of failure drove them to be extremely resourceful. As the business developed, they made a decision to move to a shop in Wallington, Surrey in order to gain a more visible High Street position. They got the cheapest rent they could find and then negotiated on the lease and furnished it with the cheapest second–hand furniture available. Because of the change in location they decided to opt for a change of name and hence Ambition 24hours was born and registered as a separate company.

Their recruitment was focused on financial services and at that time the sector was becoming much more regulated, with all financial services consultants needing to have passed exams. In order to save on advertising costs and to find the people she wanted, Marion would stand outside the exam hall and encourage candidates to join them as they left.

It was also important to keep up appearances and candidates liked to visit pleasant offices. As their office was not plush Penny used to interview all their candidates in hotel lobbies. She was regularly tapped on the shoulder by hotel staff who thought she was a prostitute plying her trade!

As the financial services industry became more regulated they decided to move into teacher recruitment, which they perceived to be the growth sector at that time. They had two sales consultants working with them and one was not the best canvasser in the world, so they asked him not to call the schools but to try some other areas, and by accident he hit on nursing homes.

WHAT HAPPENED WHEN
YOU STARTED THE JOURNEY?

Their unplanned foray into the care sector began to generate results. Suddenly there was a demand for care assistants and they were beginning to get calls at all hours of the day and even in the middle of the night! They would arrive in the office in the morning only to hear a message on their answer–phone of a customer being very apologetic and wondering if they could meet an impossible feat of finding someone in the evening. Having fought for business in the past, Penny immediately recognised a need was going unfulfilled and began to take the calls in the evening and drive staff all over the Surrey area in the middle of the night.

"On a Saturday morning at 6am I would call Marion and check that Marion's husband was waiting in his car. Marion would be in the house and Nick our consultant would get into his car, and they would all be waiting for the work to come through. As the bookings came in we would arrange to drive the staff to the customer's premises in order to fulfil the request."

They realised that this high level of customer service was bringing them business. However it did take its toll on all the staff as their contracted hours of work were 8am to 8pm. Penny would plead with them to stay longer because of the volume of calls that were coming through. Sometimes they would work until 11.30pm when they would transfer the phone line to Penny's mobile. She would take bookings at 2 or 3 o'clock in the morning and she would get nurses calling her up on a regular basis. She recalls her one nurse used to call her up every night for a chat because she thought Penny was in an office, not realising that she was actually in bed trying to get some sleep.

"We had to try and create the illusion that Ambition was a 24–hour operation because in healthcare this did not exist. Several of our competitors claimed to be available 24 hours and when we tested the market by pretending to be a nurse wishing to register, they used

to swear at us or tell us to get lost! So we knew there was a market there but it did impact on our lives – I would be going round the supermarket taking bookings because I could not bear to lose business. I was driven by the fear of what may be around the corner."

Penny even recalls the story of how during one Christmas they sat in a Chinese restaurant with seven mobile phones. They walked in with all their cardboard boxes containing the phone numbers of contacts and clients. Four of them were receiving calls and three of them were making calls to source the staff as they had not yet reached the point that they could afford the expense of running an office 24 hours a day, 7 days a week. During the meal they were on the phone so much that the restaurant owner picked up his own phone when it rang and answered, *"Ambition, can I help you?"*

Eventually Penny made the decision to go fully 24 hours because she could not stand the impact it was having on her home life. Even her children were going around saying "Ambition" and everyone walked around going *"shoosh"* all the time so that there were no distractions when calls came in. They took the top floor of the offices in Wallington, which they thought was huge at the time and decided to split the registrations and bookings. They would put the person who registered the candidates downstairs and everyone else would go upstairs and do the bookings. Penny recalls that it was quite bizarre that it was at this point they actually created their business model.

"Now that we said it would be 24 hours we had to be prepared to pay someone to sit there and do nothing if the phone did not ring. That is the hard thing. A lot of our clients did not believe that they could actually get a hold of us and it took a long time before it really justified itself. People were incredulous that they could actually get the level of service we offered. It might be that if someone rang in with a booking we would then drive round to someone's house and collect them and drop them off at the care home. Even if it's not cost effective it creates a lot of goodwill with your clients."

Penny was still driven by this fear from her past business failure and continued to be resourceful. While there was a huge demand for care assistants, it was also difficult to find suitable candidates. In the wealthier parts of Surrey, where many of their clients were located, there were no care assistants living locally. Yet there was a large immigrant community of people who had no skills and wanted jobs. So in order to meet this demand they began to run courses in the evening from their offices. Once registrations were finished downstairs they would clear away the desks and train people to become care assistants. Penny can recall people walking home from the pub past the office and wondering what was going on! This innovative approach to using the office space enabled their fixed costs to match their 24–hour model.

In order to manage their finance, they took out a factoring agreement and Penny did all the payroll and accounts. They paid everything fast, suppliers, and staff, and everyone had great service. Penny has always strong financial control of the business and up until 2001 no–one could buy a single thing without her authorisation.

Penny realised that temporary staff are often recruited at short notice and want to get their money immediately. Ambition 24hours did not have BACS payment facilities and therefore they used to have an arrangement with the bank that staff could go and cash their cheques on a Friday because many of them lived hand to mouth. As the company grew there were lines of people down the street and bank manager argued that this was no longer appropriate. Penny countered this argument by suggesting she would come into the bank and withdraw all the money in cash and then pay it to her staff!

HOW DO YOU MAINTAIN
MENTAL FITNESS AND FOCUS?

Delivering excellent service has remained at the forefront of Penny's actions. She has always taught the staff that you could be the person lying in a hospital bed and someone awful turns up so you have to deliver the level of service you would expect yourself. That service does not come cheap. Because they are able to offer last minute service they can charge a premium rate. Penny says, *"A lot of our customers say Ambition is really expensive but they never criticise the quality. It has always remained high."*

She is proud to have created a brand and model for 24–hour business and thinks that her company is well positioned to move into a number of different sectors that require this kind of service. She wants to keep growing the business and has no desire to sell. *"Initially what was driving me was money because I had none and I could not bear to think of my children sitting there and going without supper."*

One of the key factors that has enabled the business to succeed is through Penny sticking to the principles that they set out at the beginning. By not being indebted to anyone else for finance, she has been able to make decisions and live or die by them. It has given her more freedom to run the business the way she sees is appropriate.

Today, as Ambition 24hours continues to grow, the problem for those working with Penny has been that they have not always got the ability to see the same vision as she possesses. Early on they spent a lot of money on technology. They invested in a telephone system that would enable the business to grow. Penny decided to go from a five–line switchboard to a five–thousand line switchboard at a time when they only had four staff. The telephone engineer that was selling it to them commented that he thought they were going a bit overboard. Penny's response was, *"I want something that will grow with us!"* She believes you have got to be able to see the vision for growth in the future.

Another factor that helps Penny to remain motivated is her competitive instinct. She hates coming second, and combined with her fear of what may happen tomorrow, this drives her to constantly look to develop the business. She believes that the future of their business will be in retail and not just business to business. She thinks that Ambition 24hours may move into the market in some of the European hotspots where people may retire and wish to get the same high quality of care that they would do in the UK. She thinks that their reputation for service will enable them to compete effectively in this market.

In addition, with the ageing population and high levels of disposable income, she believes there will be opportunities to develop a service for high net worth private customers who want high–quality care. As they have a huge database of staff and know who the best people are, they would be in a great position to handpick them to meet the needs of the customer.

REACHING YOUR GOAL – WHAT NEXT?

Having received the accolade of Fastest Growing Business in the UK in 2002 and a turnover of over £60million, one might imagine that Penny would have slowed up the pace a little. She does admit that her work/life balance is not great and that she generally does not get home before 8.30pm but this seems a whole lot better than having the business with you 24 hours a day.

Now that finances are more secure than they were at the start in 1996, Penny measures success not only in terms of money but feedback from customers on their level of service. She remains firmly competitive and focused on the future.

Many of the staff that started out with her remain with Ambition 24hours today. She thinks it's to do with how they have organised the work within the company. "*I think it's because people feel they can cope. Our consultants never interview anyone, it's all done by registration officers. I looked at the model for a normal nursing agency and thought you can't be sitting there interviewing someone and having to fill bookings and requirements on the phone at the same time. The commercial pressure does not marry up with compliance.*"

Whatever Ambition 24hours looks like in the future one thing is certain. Penny Streeter will be singularly focused and determined on making it a success. It's amazing how the fear of failure can be such a powerful driver to help one succeed. I for one have no doubt that she will achieve whatever she puts her mind to.

PENNY STREETER'S TOP TIPS

◊ Keep your cash in your pocket and manage the finances carefully

◊ Don't make the mistake of thinking you need lots of money to grow your business – you don't. We started buying second–hand furniture and still follow that philosophy today

◊ Invest in technology that can grow with you early on

Helen Swaby

FOUNDER AND MANAGING DIRECTOR OF DEMONTFORT FINE ART

The UK's leading fine art publisher and distributor of original paintings

www.tinahadley.com

Key Information

Business: Fine art publisher and distributor of original paintings

Started business: 1995

Location: Lichfield, Staffordshire

Turnover in 2004: £7.1 million

Employees: 65

Awards include: Recognised as one of the Fastest Growing companies in 2002 by Fast Track 100

Website: www.demontfortfineart.co.uk

WHAT WAS THE DEFINING MOMENT?

It's perhaps not surprising that after being brought up in an environment of entrepreneurship Helen Swaby used this ethos to successfully turn her hobby into a multi–million pound art publishing business.

Her father was a very successful entrepreneur who had left school at 14, started a business and turned it into a public company with a £50 million turnover. "*He was a very driven man, incredibly focused and charismatic.*"

On the other hand Helen describes her mother as "*my best pal and the most caring and sensitive individual I know*", which gave her two contrasting role models.

Instilled into her at an early age were the strong family values of honesty, integrity and morality, which Helen believes are intrinsic to where she is now. At school, Helen was extremely competitive and excelled both in sports and academically. At university she studied psychology which has helped her to understand what motivates and drives people in the business environment.

Helen's first job was in the agricultural market, where she worked successfully as an agent for a company with a £1 million turnover. Her success in sales helped this to increase within 3 years to £5 million. She describes her sales technique as a bit "*outlandish*" compared to others in the company, using her outgoing nature and good humour to go in to a client and say, "*Hello, Mr ... how about a big order today?"* Putting her people skills to good use meant that she was able to effectively build good working relationships with her clients, something that is also an asset for her in DeMontfort Fine Art. Helen quickly developed her confidence and was rewarded with a substantial salary.

This enabled her to buy a small cottage, and when furnishing it, Helen decided that she needed some artwork for the walls. So she went in search of a few pieces. By chance there was a small art publishing company in the village where she lived and when Helen walked in the girl behind the counter agreed to sell her some art at trade prices.

Helen then decided to buy a few additional pieces to hold an art party where she would sell them to her friends. *"They would arrive and we would have a few drinks and they were very willing to buy the pieces. Sometimes they would spend around £5000 in a weekend. The great thing was, it was the product that inspired me."*

This got Helen hooked and while travelling around the country for her agricultural job she would pop into local galleries and look at the artwork. As a complete novice she quickly learnt about the subject, having not had experience of attending art societies or working in an art gallery. *"I did not know what a limited edition was until I bought my first two in a gallery in Birmingham."*

So she set about getting together a very modest portfolio of artists who would sell their work to her at £50 or so and rang a gallery in Birmingham and asked if she could go and show them the lovely artwork she had. *"I remember leaving the gallery with an order of about £500 and as I got out of the gallery I punched the air as I thought it was so fantastic."* This was the key defining moment for Helen, because if the owner had criticised her offerings, she probably would have given up. So she looked up more galleries in the Yellow Pages and began travelling about selling her artwork. This business earned an annual turnover of £15,000, and the profits added to the income from her day job.

WHAT WAS THE MARKET SITUATION AND YOUR PERSONAL SITUATION AT START–UP?

After years of running the artwork business as a hobby Helen eventually decided to give up the well–paid agricultural job and run her own business on a full–time basis. She knew deep down that her passion was for art and therefore she would have to follow her heart. *"If you really enjoy something, you can work with more fervour, enthusiasm and passion."*

Her business initially ran out of the stable block at her parents' home. Helen purchased a small red van and in no time employed an assistant. One of them would travel to galleries in the van with all the portfolios and the other would work in the office. Helen used her gut feeling to select artwork that she believed would sell in the galleries. *"I just thought if I loved it then everyone else would love it too. Sometimes the artwork was a bit more contemporary than they were used to but we encouraged the galleries to buy it. Their customers would buy it and they would call us up and want some more from that artist. It was self–perpetuating and grew out of nothing in a sense."*

WHAT WAS YOUR COMPELLING VISION?

There is a common misconception that buying art is something for the elite few. When Helen started out she wanted to provide contemporary yet accessible images for everyone and while the company has grown over the years she has never lost sight of this initial goal.

Helen realised that her company needed to help the retail outlets sell their work. So they worked closely with their retailing partners to create a unique package of marketing support. That meant DeMontfort Fine Art not only provided the artwork for sale, but marketing materials to go along with it, which makes the art gallery owner's job easier. This helps maximise sales and the profile of Helen's company.

As DeMontfort Fine Art has expanded, the importance of communicating this vision has become even more vital to ensure that all staff understand the aims and desires of the business before they join.

HOW DID YOU PREPARE FOR SUCCESS?

Customer service has always been at the forefront of what Helen strives to achieve. Even when speaking to her one gets the impression of her desire to please. *"When customers place an order with us we thank them for the business and find out what else we can do for them. We can help them with their marketing, or arrange an event or whatever, it's not just sign the order and thanks, goodbye."* Even other companies in the industry have adopted some of their practices because they have recognised the value of it.

Another factor that Helen believes has been critical to their success is their people. 85% of the workforce is female, and in Helen's experience, *"women are phenomenal workers who can use their wily charms and personality to get great orders from the client."* She is a very hands–on leader and ensures they have lots of meetings and communication to ensure there is a feel–good factor in the company. Attitude and enthusiasm is everything in the business, and Helen will take no short–cuts when recruiting staff. *"I tell everyone I need a very positive attitude because we are a positive forward–thinking company and if you do not have it you will not fit in here."*

The company has a relatively low turnover of staff probably because they are well looked after. If someone is not up to the job, then Helen will talk it through with them and redirect or refocus them, working closely to ensure success.

WHAT HAPPENED WHEN
YOU STARTED THE JOURNEY?

As for many of the other women in this book, the issue of finance has been a challenge for Helen at times. Yet she firmly believes that the best way to address it is to develop a strong relationship with your bank manager. *"Show them what you do and get them involved so that they feel part of your business. It's much easier to work with someone who has an understanding of the challenges you face."*

They also had to deal with a litigation case which brought out Helen's strong family values of honesty and integrity. The case related to an infringement of copyright where one of their main artists' works was being copied by another artist. It was a journey into an unknown territory of injunctions, legal arguments and barristers which Helen would have rather avoided.

However, she firmly believed that if they took on an artist, they had a duty to protect them. *"What is the point in having a publishing company with artists assigning their copyright to me if it means nothing? I firmly believe that I am not just protecting the artist but my business, my staff and my other artists."* It was a tough process which involved huge expense and investment of time and became a test case in their industry. Eventually it was settled out of court but it did firmly test Helen's personal values.

Helen also sees her role as providing inspiration and motivation for her artists. *"We don't just take their artwork and say thanks and publish it; a lot of work goes on behind the scenes where we talk about trends, colours, styles and designs. It is a very time–consuming process for me but I am here to inspire them to paint great imagery which they might never have imagined was possible. Artists can be very isolated individuals and we are often their only form of contact with the outside world. They need to be inspired to produce their best results and we are providing them with feedback on their work from the marketplace."*

It's a rapidly changing market that Helen operates in. DeMontfort Fine Art launches around 150 new images 3 times a year, printed as limited editions at each publishing in spring, summer and autumn. Therefore there is pressure to ensure artists are on top of their game at all times. The investment that Helen makes in motivating the artists obviously has a bottom–line business benefit at the end of the day. The company also provides a level of security for the artists who trust that they will get their regular payments each month and are confident that the company is doing what they are really good at – which is marketing their artwork.

HOW DO YOU MAINTAIN
MENTAL FITNESS AND FOCUS?

Helen admits that she does find it hard to maintain a work/life balance. As the business grows she pushes herself to the limit, working late into the night and taking no time to relax. Yet, as many of the other women entrepreneurs recognise, it is not possible to achieve success without hard work and making sacrifices.

Even today Helen still works long hours but has found a fantastic partner who has helped her to bring an element of balance to her life. *"It's not easy finding someone who can cope with a successful woman because men perceive it as intimidating. They worry about the power and that I might be a control freak or demanding and domineering. Yet I get out of work and I show a different side to my character. At work I have to be tough with suppliers but I am sympathetic. Yet deep down I am sensitive and caring. I care about my team and if they have problems I am the first one to be there for them. My friends also bring out my nurturing side. I value being there to offer relationship advice and to encourage them to get the best out of their lives."*

Building up a strong team in the workplace is also a strategy that Helen is using to help her bring more balance to her life. *"The more I get a strong team around me the more I can delegate. The team comes up with great ideas and they inspire me. It's no longer about me as the person who created the company but about the team which is creating the future."*

Helen is also well aware of the impact that her mood has on the rest of the staff. Even if she is feeling despondent, she recognises that as a leader she needs to maintain a positive outlook all the time to help others through their tough times. Yet the downside is, who is there to pat Helen on the head and say well done? She says that this comes from the feedback from clients and artists who appreciate the great job that we do for them. *"That's what gives me a buzz."*

REACHING YOUR GOAL – WHAT NEXT?

Success for Helen is around what she has accomplished over time. She has a sense of pride, recognising that she set out not knowing the marketplace, and over the years she has built up a business that provides a great working environment for her employees and artists. DeMontfort is now recognised as the UK's leading fine art publisher and distributor of original paintings.

Yet her ambition does not stop there. Helen is filled with new ideas for the future and is armed with a great team and her own determination, focus and massive attention to detail. I have no doubt that she will achieve even greater success.

When asked to choose a favourite career moment Helen typically mentions the success of one of her artists. Doug Hyde was recently named the UK's official best selling artist by the Fine Art Trade Guild, and was described in a BBC national news report as "the most popular living artist in the UK." Hyde's extraordinary rise from virtual unknown (pre DeMontfort) to this exalted position as the UK's number 1 artist has been meteoric, and his stunning Original Pastels and Limited Edition Prints have become genuine collectors' items.

'Bear Hug' by Doug Hyde

Although his natural talent is exceptional, in the competitive art market it takes imagination, experience and commercial acumen to get an artist noticed, so his success is in a large degree attributable to Helen's outstanding abilities. One of the reasons why she is so proud of this particular achievement is that in many ways Hyde represents everything she stands for – quality artwork with massive appeal at affordable prices.

HELEN SWABY'S TOP TIPS

◊ Be a realist and recognise that success does not happen overnight

◊ Believe in yourself and have confidence in your own abilities

◊ Enjoy the journey and be prepared to make sacrifices

◊ Make sure you create a strong support system in family, friends or a partner. You want to be with people who are encouraging you

◊ Set pragmatic goals. You don't have to be a high flying entrepreneur to get pleasure out of life. There is life after work

Yvonne Thompson CBE

FOUNDER AND MANAGING DIRECTOR OF ASAP COMMUNICATIONS

Created the European Federation of Black Women Business Owners

Key Information

Business: PR and communications

Started business: 1983

Location: London

Turnover in 2003: £750,000

Employees: 5

Awards include: Awarded a CBE in the Queen's Birthday Honours List in 2003 in recognition of her work with black and ethnic minority businesses. Winner of the British Section of the European Union of Women awards in 2001, Businessperson of the Year Award by Voice newspaper.

Website: www.efbwbo.net

WHAT WAS THE DEFINING MOMENT?

While working in the record industry, Yvonne Thompson shrewdly spotted the gap in the market that was to set her off on the road to entrepreneurship. Yet the decision to take that step came as a result of repeated disappointment when trying to get promoted. Having worked in CBS Records for over seven years and gaining considerable experience the crunch point came when she had been standing in as the Head of Press. When the vacancy was advertised Yvonne did not get the job. This happened to her three times and on the last occasion Yvonne made the decision that the only way to move up was to move on.

WHAT WAS THE MARKET SITUATION AND YOUR PERSONAL SITUATION AT START–UP?

Yvonne's career was originally destined to be in nursing. Her sister had followed in her parent's footsteps and everyone assumed she would make the same career choice. In fact she began the pre–nursing course and was working at the same time for Nat West Bank earning £12 per week, which was considered to be extremely good in the 1970s. It was the prospect of reducing her standard of living initially that pushed Yvonne to turn her back on nursing, to remain in corporate life.

She gave birth to her daughter in 1975 and could not face going back into banking, so looked for something more exciting. Luckily, finding a temporary job in Phonogram suited her perfectly and she was to remain there for 2 ½ years. As a secretary in copyright and contracts Yvonne gained valuable experience in the legal and technical side of the music business and shortly after she moved over to take on the role of Junior Press Officer. This gave Yvonne the excitement she craved because it involved dealing with radio, TV and press contacts, as well as with the music artists themselves.

From there she moved to CBS Records where she was repeatedly overlooked for promotion. It was rare at that time to have black people working in record companies, let alone black females, so it was an uphill struggle for Yvonne. After the third refusal she ran into the ladies toilet, cried her eyes out, went back to her desk and handed in her notice.

At this time Yvonne began to notice that there were a lot of independent press officers (PRs) in the music industry representing white bands but none existed for black bands. Generally, black bands did not feature much in the music industry in the 1970s and record companies tended only to work with those that were already established names. So those that did come from the USA arrived without any independent press officer – a prerequisite to promote their music to the media. Ironically, many of the most popular acts in today's music charts are black artists which shows how much things have changed in 20 years.

The role of a press officer in a record company was to represent 15 or 20 bands at a time, which meant it was only when a record was scheduled for release that a band tended to get any attention. Consequently many bands opted to employ independent PRs who could devote a greater level of attention to them individually.

WHAT WAS YOUR COMPELLING VISION?

Now that Yvonne was a free agent and knew her way around the business she decided to set up her own company because she believed that she could do a better job than the independent PRs that she knew. She also knew that as a black woman she would be able to effectively represent the black bands and effectively exploit this gap in the market.

All her friends and family did not believe that she could do it and thought that she would miss all the free T–shirts and tickets to gigs that she had got in her previous job.

It was a huge risk for her because her daughter was now seven years old and she felt a great level of responsibility to ensure that she kept food on the table and a roof over their head. But she ignored the negative voices inside her head and kept focusing on what she believed she could achieve.

HOW DID YOU PREPARE FOR SUCCESS?

Her first break came when she was able to barter desk space in the offices of the Independent Record Labels

Association in return for doing their PR. This also gave her access to over 300 record labels that were members of the Association. She offered members a preferential rate to do their PR and ended up winning a lot of business, including working with CBS, her old employer! It also enabled her business to have a West End address to add credibility and gave her easy day–to–day access to that area of London, which is where all the action was.

WHAT HAPPENED WHEN
YOU STARTED THE JOURNEY?

As her business grew, Yvonne worked regularly for London's Capital Radio, promoting their annual music festival. From this they were looking for someone to work on their black music concerts and more importantly on an event called "Reggae Sunsplash" which was a big reggae concert that happens in Jamaica. Capital Radio wanted to bring it to the UK and this was a huge piece of work. Yvonne landed the contract and it was the beginning of a project that was repeated for four years.

One of the greatest challenges she encountered as a single mother in the early days was balancing the needs of work and her daughter. Yvonne acknowledges that she gave her daughter a lot of responsibility from the age of seven. *"She was, and still is an independent thinker. Although she was meant to go to the babysitter after school she would decide to go home because she had her own key and preferred her own company. Then the babysitter would call me wondering where she was. My daughter would call me and say I am at home, can I make some toast? I would then feel awful worrying about her and feeling I should be there for her. Eventually you learn to trust that your child is actually quite sensible and can take care of herself to a certain extent and you have to allow her that responsibility.*

One day she opened the electricity bill and said she was worried about how we would pay for it. My reaction was to reassure her that I would take responsibility for those things if she took responsibility for doing well at school."

From the music industry Yvonne began to move into doing PR for "serious things". She recognised that while the music industry was glamorous, you were only as good as your last hit unless you got a long–term contract with a management company. Her business moved into a wide variety of areas including theatre, book launches, hair–care and fashion. She needed to find more stable income streams and these were more likely to be found in the corporate or public sector environments.

Growing the business also meant taking on staff, and similarly to Penny Streeter, Yvonne believes that you need to treat people the way you would like to be treated. *"I think we are fairly relaxed and we don't have strict rules but I do insist on timekeeping. There is no hierarchy as such which enables us to be extremely flexible in our work with clients."*

ASAP Communications has been very successful for over twenty years in winning clients who wanted to target the black community. Today the client list includes The Dome, BA, Choice FM, Corporation of London and The Voice newspaper. The company has grown, and a lot of its success has been down the Yvonne's personal reputation.

Yet financial success was not what motivated Yvonne. She also felt the need personally to work on something that was more meaningful to her. She found herself reviewing her personal values and creating a plan that was going to help her find greater personal satisfaction from her work. Yvonne began to get more involved in working in the community, helping to give organisations access to minority audiences and communities. *"They are hard to reach for others but not for me."*

In 1997 she also started up the European Federation of Black Women Business Owners because there appeared to be a lack of role models or like–minded black business women that she could network with or ask to be her mentor.

HOW DO YOU MAINTAIN
MENTAL FITNESS AND FOCUS?

One of the qualities that Yvonne believes has helped her succeed is having focus and a clear vision of what she wants to do. *"It's important not to be swayed by other people's advice and that you are able to make decisions yourself. When I became part of the founding group for Choice FM –*

the first 24 hour soul music radio station– everyone was saying we would never get a licence but I was quite determined. It was the best thing I have ever done."

It's this kind of more purposeful work that Yvonne has found satisfying over the years. She is now a Board member of Britain in Europe, an Observer on the Board of Business Link for London, and a member of the DTI's Small Business Council. In addition she also chairs the DTI's Ethnic Minority Business Forum and the London Central Learning and Skills Council, as well as serving as President of the European Federation of Black Women Business Owners. Yvonne was awarded a CBE in the Queen's Birthday Honours List in 2003 in recognition of the work she has carried out with black and ethnic minority businesses.

"This is so much more rewarding. It makes me feel good because I know it can be hard work at times but I feel I have done something worthwhile. I have always been interested in helping people but it's just in the last few years it has happened to be higher profile."

As a self–confessed workaholic she finds it hard to take long holidays. Until recently she owned a house in Cornwall that she visited on alternate weekends but found it a long haul. Her daughter is now grown up and living in Germany so she tries to visit her regularly.

REACHING YOUR GOAL – WHAT NEXT?

Reflecting back on her experiences over the last 20 years or so Yvonne would have liked to have taken the opportunity for some higher education at an earlier stage in her life as this could have helped her in business.

She recognises that she has been a pioneer for black women in the PR industry. *"When I started the company in 1983 PR Week did an article on me. They carried out some research and found that there were no other black–owned PR companies in London. That is not so long ago. There have been many firsts that I have achieved, but it's quite lonely along the way and it's only in the last 10 years that there have been any support networks for black businesswomen."*

Finding an exit strategy is difficult for Yvonne. She realises that without her involvement ASAP Communications would not be as valuable to a possible purchaser. *"If I had found a suitable business partner I would have been able to step back and the partners could continue. I did have two partners throughout the time and it just did not work out for various reasons and it's a bruising experience. It's like having a divorce and you cannot do that too many times. But ASAP is really Yvonne Thompson. People buy me."*

YVONNE THOMPSON'S TOP TIPS

◊ Know what you want to achieve in your business
◊ Be known for doing it
◊ Be focused and determined
◊ Have the ability to make your own decisions and not be swayed by others
◊ Be brave enough to jump in and do it!

PART 2: APPLYING THE SEVEN STEPS TO SUCCESS™

You Can Do It Too

Having read all these awe–inspiring accounts of how these women began their businesses you will no doubt be wondering how you can also build your own entrepreneurial dreams. That's where the *Seven Steps to Success*™ come in handy. This chapter is your own guide to the steps you need to take to start up your own business venture. It enables you to apply the learning from the entrepreneurs' stories while following a structured framework to help focus your thoughts and ideas.

Seven Steps to Success™

Always start with the end in mind – what do you want to achieve?

Step 1 – The Defining Moment

Step 2 – Understand Your Environment

Step 3 – Create Your Own Compelling Vision

Step 4 – Prepare for Success

Step 5 – Start the Journey

Step 6 – Maintain Fitness and Focus

Step 7 – Reach Your Goal – What Next?

STEP 1 – THE DEFINING MOMENT

It is vital to reflect on what has prompted you to start up a business. This is often particularly important later on in the journey when the going, as it invariably does, gets tough, because it helps to remind you why you decided to start up in the first place. Ask yourself these questions:

What is *inspiring* me to start up in business?

1. Do I have the desire to control my own destiny?

2. Am I interested in making a lot of money?

3. Do I want to make a difference?

4. Have I identified a gap in the market?

5. Am I passionate about a product or service?

What is *forcing* to me start up my own business?

1. Have I been made redundant?

2. Am I returning to work after a career break and looking for flexibility?

3. Have I reached a glass ceiling in my career?

4. Do I find few opportunities to be creative and innovative?

5. Am I sick of the corporate treadmill?

If you have answered "yes" to more of the questions in the first category, it is likely that the attractiveness of running your own business is pulling you towards that option. If on the other hand your "yes" responses tend to be more in the second category it is likely that you are being pushed towards entrepreneurship perhaps because the more conventional approach of being employed does not seem as appealing to you.

Regardless of whether you feel you are being pushed or pulled to being an entrepreneur, there are still a number of factors that you will have overcome in order to get started. These factors include accessing start–up finance, maintaining a level of confidence, having the right knowledge and skills, finding the right support team and selecting an appropriate type of business to start.

However, having read the accounts of the successful women entrepreneurs in the preceding chapters, you should now have a clearer idea of how to overcome many of these obstacles.

STEP 2 – UNDERSTAND YOUR ENVIRONMENT

It is important that you become aware of what is going on in the current business environment as well as understanding your own personal circumstances. This will help you identify if it is the right time for you to start up.

Carry out an assessment of the market environment from the viewpoint of your business, competitors and potential customers. Be sure to take into consideration the current external factors that might either help or hinder you in starting–up.

Understanding your environment

1. **Social** – What are the changing habits, trends or consumer behaviours in society?

2. **Technological** – How will changing technology affect your business idea?

3. **Economic** – How are the current states of the economy, interest rates, taxation etc. likely to have an impact?

4. **Environmental** – Are issues related to location, environment and weather relevant?

5. **Political** – Does current government policy and the law make a difference?

Then consider how your personal circumstances might help or hinder you. While many of the women in the book found ways to overcome obstacles related to accessing finance or looking after children it is important to think about all the circumstances that might be relevant.

Assessing your personal circumstances

◊   Do I have enough money to get started?

◊   Have I got responsibilities for children or dependents?

◊   Do my family or friends support me?

◊   Do I live in the appropriate location?

◊   Can I cope with a lot of setbacks?

◊   Will my cultural background or religious beliefs impact on my business?

◊   Have I got time to do this?

◊   Am I prepared to make sacrifices?

Be honest with yourself. There is no point in pretending to yourself that everything will be okay, if you know deep down that there is an issue that is likely to stop you. If you do identify any possible problem areas, either find a way to resolve them or take the decision that perhaps now is not the right time for you to take this step. There are lots of ways to get support through this stage. All entrepreneurs who are running established businesses will have gone through this and there are lots of business support agencies and organisations who have people who can provide advice, support and an unbiased opinion to help you assess all the critical factors.

STEP 3 – CREATE YOUR COMPELLING VISION

An essential part of the leadership of a business is based on creating a compelling vision. This is a descriptive statement of what your business will be like at a specified time in the future, and is likely to use words, phrases or even pictures to describe what you expect to see, hear and experience at that time.

In order to do this, you need to connect with your "inner self" in order to understand your deepest personal dreams and passions. This in turn releases energy and excitement about life and where you're heading. This will give you a natural magnetism as such passion arouses enthusiasm in others.

To create your vision, close your eyes and imagine yourself being transported to a time in the future when your business is running successfully. Think about the following...

Creating your compelling vision

◊   What will be happening?

◊   Who will be there with you?

◊   How will other people be describing your business?

◊   What emotions will you be feeling?

◊   What will it feel like?

◊   How much money will you have?

Now draw a picture, or write down some words or phrases to describe what you have imagined. Bring your vision to life by thinking about the colours, the noise and the feelings that you will be experiencing. You may find that the vision is unclear when you start out, but becomes clearer as you progress with your business. That's okay because it may only be through learning and experience that you are able to create a more powerful and compelling vision.

However, your vision alone will not be enough. You will have to persuade others – customers, partners, employees, suppliers and the bank manager to see it, share it and support it. And it will be your ability to communicate the vision that will be a key factor in your success.

Whatever vision you create, it is likely to be based on your own personal values. These are the principles that guide your thinking and actions and are the standards that we use to judge ourselves and others. For example, if we value honesty, we expect others to be honest too.

In the successful businesses in this book, the personal values of the women had a profound influence on the way they ran their companies and the decisions they made. For example, Helen Swaby values honesty and integrity. She demonstrated that it was important when she pursued the legal case on behalf of one of her artists regardless of the cost involved.

Every day, use your vision to keep you focused. You must try to imagine that your vision *is* reality rather than thinking it has yet to be achieved. I created a powerful vision for myself every time I wanted to achieve a challenging goal and I made sure that it remained a strong image in my head, compelling me towards it.

STEP 4 – PREPARE FOR SUCCESS

This step involves preparation of a plan to achieve the vision over a specific timescale. You need to consider the following...

Preparing for success

◊ Writing a business plan

◊ Finding the finance required

◊ Writing down a list of all the people or organisations that could help you and then approaching them for help and support

◊ Obtaining relevant experience, skills or training

◊ Finding a location to start up

◊ Developing personal discipline to stick to your plan

◊ Writing a list of all the obstacles that might stop you and thinking about how to get round them

◊ Reading books about other successful business people to learn from them

---

During this planning stage, it is also beneficial to consider what your "exit" strategy might be for the business.

o Do you want to build a lifestyle business that will offer you flexibility?

o Do you want to grow a business to sell it in the future?

o Do you want to grow a business that you can run in the future?

If you are in a position to answer this question then it will help you to determine the direction that the business takes over the coming months and years.

STEP 5 – START THE JOURNEY

This is the implementation phase. You need to be 100% committed, prepared to make mistakes, take risks and to learn along the way. Soon after you start, reality will hit and there are many challenges that you will need to overcome...

Financial issues

Managing cash flow is the biggest challenge for any small business in the first year. When you start trading you will have to spend money on making and selling your products before you receive any income from sales.

It can sometimes be up to 120 days between paying suppliers for materials and receiving payment from customers. This time delay is what can put many companies out of business before they even get started.

Make sure you understand the difference between profit and cash. You can still be profitable but run out of cash. Find a good accountant or bookkeeper and make sure you develop a sound working relationship with your bank manager. Keep them informed if problems arise, as they are much more likely to be supportive if you are open and honest with them.

Charging what you are worth

This is particularly an issue for women in a service business, as they can be reluctant to charge the market rate for their services because they feel they are not "worth it". But if you don't value your time, then why should a customer pay? It's much harder to increase your prices once you have begun to get a reputation for not charging full price, so learn to negotiate from the outset and recognise your own value.

Working from home

Many people find that they cannot switch off from work, particularly if they are home–based. Try to separate an area for your workspace that you can shut off or close from the rest of your home in the evening. That way you can create a physical barrier between home and work.

Develop other methods of separating home and work too. For example have different telephone lines, use your computer only for work during the day, actually leave your house in the morning and go for a walk before starting work.

Working in isolation

It can be lonely if you start up a business from home and you have been used to a busy office environment. If you find that you are becoming isolated, take steps to address the issue. Go to local networking events and meet other like–minded people. You can then arrange to call or meet up with them on a regular basis. Plan to make phone calls every day to ensure that you speak to someone or visit the gym to exercise and meet people.

Measuring progress

When you start up it can be easy to get caught up in the day to day work and lose sight of the progress you are making. Ensure that you carry out a quick review at the end of each week or month to assess the progress you have made towards your vision. It can help to keep you motivated as well as focused.

Feast and famine

One problem that many sole traders encounter is the issue of sporadic amounts of work, and therefore income. They get a few clients and are extremely busy and therefore have no time to do any marketing for the next quiet spell. Try to identify periods when you think that work may be quieter and make sure that you keep yourself occupied with worthwhile work during this time. It can be tempting to take time off or become undisciplined if you do not have regular commitments, so use this time wisely to focus on important jobs like updating your website, or sending out a newsletter to customers. Make sure you have kept enough money from the busy times to pay for your regular financial commitments during these quiet periods.

Bartering

Most people do not have huge amounts of cash available at start up to pay for the services that they require such as creating a website, preparing marketing materials or employing a book–keeper. Bartering has become an accepted method of operating in recent years and can be useful when you cannot afford to pay for services. If you do agree to barter with a supplier then make sure that you negotiate and agree an outcome that is acceptable to both parties.

STEP 6 – MAINTAIN FITNESS AND FOCUS

As you get used to running your own business, day–to-day issues may crop up that cause you stress and sap your energy. It is important to ensure you set aside some time to relax and recuperate. There are various ways that you can achieve this...

Maintaining fitness and focus

- Take time to exercise and get enough sleep

- Eat healthily and drink lots of water

- Plan some time in each day to sit quietly or meditate

- Reward yourself for progress towards your vision with a small treat

- Make time to do some deep breathing and stretching

- Refocus your mind on the goal that you are working towards

If your partner or spouse is working in the business with you, then it is even more important to find ways of separating work and home life. Set aside time regularly for both of you to have a "date" together. Make sure you avoid talking about work!

If you have caring or domestic responsibilities, then recognise that you cannot be the perfect mum or carer if you are trying to start up a business. Be realistic in recognising what you can achieve and then make sure that you try to stick to it.

Finding a mentor

It is also useful to find a person who can act as a mentor. They can provide an independent viewpoint and help you to maintain focus. The best place to look for a mentor is right in front of you. Is there an individual who you admire and respect? Someone who has always impressed you with their insight and perceptiveness?

Maybe it could be someone you have read about or met at a business event. It could even be an older individual who isn't currently a business leader in your sector, but who you know has lots of experience.

Approach that individual and ask if they would consider being your mentor. Depending on the individual, and your current relationship, your proposal will vary in the amount of detail and how it is delivered. At the very least, let them know why you selected them and what you hope to learn from the association. If appropriate for the specific individual, you can also discuss amounts of time to be committed and what you will contribute.

Even if they decline to be your mentor, and few will, they will be flattered to have been asked and will surely become a loyal supporter.

STEP 7 – REACH YOUR GOAL – WHAT NEXT?

How will you know that you have achieved success? Identify what success means to you. It might be in terms of financial results, customer satisfaction, building a brand, penetration of a market or maintaining the values of your business. Once you have decided, set up a system for monitoring progress towards your goals.

Once you reach a level of success yourself, then you may consider also giving something back to others in business. You could become a mentor to others starting out or sharing your experiences in some way to help others.

I have also found it useful to consider what my next goal is before I achieve the one I am working on. That way, you lessen the emotional dip between goals that you can experience if you achieve something really difficult and then think "what next?"

What is really most important is that you enjoy the journey. Running a business can be extremely satisfying and provide an opportunity for you to control your own destiny. The stories in this book have illustrated the highs and the lows that ten successful businesswomen have encountered. I hope that they have provided you with inspiration and motivation to get out there and start up your own business too. Enjoy your journey!

ABOUT THE AUTHOR

 Sue Stockdale is a motivational speaker, successful business woman and a record breaking explorer. Following a corporate career in training, she founded Mission Possible in 1997, specialising in motivation, entrepreneurship and leadership. She has made a major impact with a wide variety of clients, typically working at director or senior management level.

Sue is passionate about women's enterprise and is on the Board of several organisations related to business start–up. She delivers workshops and lectures on the subject across Europe.

In addition, Sue was the first British Woman to walk to the Magnetic North Pole in 1996 and has represented Scotland in athletics and cross–country events. She also finished runner–up in the Channel 4 show *Superhuman*.

She holds a Masters Degree in Quality Management and Improvement, an MBA in Entrepreneurship and Business Venturing and was awarded an Enterprise Fellowship from Oxford Brookes University in 2005.

Sue's advice regularly appears in the media and her first book, *Kickstart Your Motivation* received favourable reviews.

Speaking engagements and workshops can be booked at www.missionpossible.co.uk

USEFUL RESOURCES

Brady, K (2004) Playing to Win, Capstone Publishing

Brush, Carter, Gatewood, Greene & Hart (2004) Clearing the Hurdles: Women building high–growth businesses, Prentice Hall

Burns, P & Morris, P (1995) Pocket Guide to Business Finance, Butterworth–Heinemann

Craven, R (2001) Kickstart your Business, Virgin Publishing

Franks, L (2000) The Seed Handbook, Thorsons

Gerber, M (1994) The E Myth Revisited, HarperCollins

Hashemi, Sahar and Bobby (2003) Anyone Can Do It, Capstone Publishing

Jenkins, D & Gregory, J (2003) The Gorillas Want Bananas: The Lean Marketing Handbook for Small Expert Businesses, Lean Marketing Press

Parks, S (2004) Start your Business: Week by Week, Prentice Hall

Southon, M & West, C (2002) The Beermat Entrepreneur, Prentice Hall

Stockdale, S (2002) Kickstart your Motivation, J Wiley & Sons

Woods, C (2003) From Acorns...How to Build your Brilliant Business from Scratch, Prentice Hall

MISSION **POSS**|BLE

Mission Possible. Make it happen.

- Achieve a goal that you think is impossible
- Get help to start up or grow a business
- Follow the Seven Steps to Success™ programme

It is our belief that everyone has the capability to achieve what they want to – often the only person stopping them is themselves.

We deliver motivational presentations that inspire, motivate and energise people to take action.

We work with business leaders, executives and teams to help them focus on what they want to achieve, understand what is stopping them and identify ways to overcome those obstacles to success.

We also work with owner–managers and people want to start–up in business by providing workshops, networking and a website resource of information.

As a result our clients have:
- Started up in business
- Improved their levels of confidence
- Recognised new opportunities
- Maximised their resources, talents and capabilities
- Learned new concepts and techniques
- Felt more motivated and energised
- Achieved improved performance

...and that is just the start!

To find out more contact Mission Possible Ltd
Tel: +44 (0)1367 244855
Email: info@missionpossible.co.uk
Website: www.missionpossible.co.uk

PRAISE

"Sue Stockdale has produced a gem of a book here. From experience of helping over 100,000 start ups a year and from our research, we know just how important role models are in inspiring people to start in business. In Secrets of Successful Women Entrepreneurs, Sue has complemented that with practical advice that would be helpful even to those who've been in business for years."

Stephen Pegge
Head of Commmunications, Lloyds TSB Business Banking

"These portraits don't just tell a business story, they tell how it really feels to be an entrepreneur, from the depths of near-despair to the moments of elation when the original passion and insights become a successful brand. Each of Sue's short, insightful, honest and well-formatted portraits is inspirational reading for early stage entrepreneurs."

Margaret Milan
President of European Professional Women's Network and founder of "Eveil & Jeux", France's leading educational toy company

"The biographies of these successful women entrepreneurs were illuminating. Sue Stockdale has selected some inspirational women to profile and she offers practical advice for women wanting to start in business."

Professor Sara Carter
Hunter Centre for Entrepreneurship, University of Strathclyde

"These are no ordinary women - this is no ordinary book. The Secrets of Successful Women Entrepreneurs exposes the lives of great business women allowing the reader to glimpse behind the business curtain to observe the virtues, intolerable obstacles and tenacity which is at the heart of any entrepreneurial enterprise."

Maria Kempinska
Creative Chairman, Jongleurs Comedy Ltd

"The book is the next best thing to having a life-time of role-models for the next generation of successful women entrepreneurs. Sue Stockdale has hit on a 'do-it-yourself' model for entrepreneurship and it works!"

Candace Johnson

International Telecommunications Entrepreneur behind SES ASTRA, Teleport Europe, Europe Online and countless other companies throughout the world

"Clearly, businesswomen are not a homogenous group; however, these stories reflect our research indicating that women tend to prefer to minimise and closely manage debt and are extremely well prepared by the time they approach banks or investors. They also recognise that large scale success does demand some personal sacrifice."

Clare Logie

Director, Women in Business, Bank of Scotland

"Sue Stockdale uncovers the Secrets of Successful Women Entrepreneurs with her latest book. Her accounts of successful women provide clear examples to other would-be entrepreneurs on overcoming obstacles. Her true stories are straight talking and sensible and Stockdale urges the reader to be honest and have a compelling vision for their venture and their entrepreneurial life. The accounts stress how these ten women have achieved a presence to be successful. As an entrepreneurship educator at Dalton State College in the United States and Director of the Center for Applied Business Studies, I work with many individuals, writing their business plans and beginning their own companies. Sue's book is right on target in its application of universal entrepreneurial principles and her refreshing writing style assures the readers understand the new venture creation process. In each of the ten accounts of the UK entrepreneurs, Stockdale's 'Seven Steps to Success' are highlighted. While the stories may be from women in the United Kingdom, the principles are universal to all start-ups. I definitely recommend Sue's book as required reading for anyone considering self employment."

Dr. Marilyn M. Helms, CFPIM, CIRM

Sesquicentennial Endowed Chair and Professor of Management and Director, Center for Applied Business Studies, Dalton State College, Georgia, USA

Want to live the business dream?

Feel
free

Starting up a new business? That's when every penny really does count. At HSBC, we recognise that it's your money that's supporting your business, that's why our Business Account is designed to help preserve your funds. So you'll get 12 months' banking absolutely free, plus access to a business specialist to answer any of your questions, and more. We give you the support – you make it happen.

- Free – 12 months' banking
- Free – Business Card for first year
- Free access to our award-winning 24/7 internet banking service

▶ Call 0800 587 1585
▶ Click hsbc.co.uk/business
▶ Come into your local branch

HSBC ◆X◆
The world's local bank

Lightning Source UK Ltd.
Milton Keynes UK
UKOW020638210112

185783UK00001B/15/A